High Heaven

HIGH HEAVEN

by Jacques Boell

INTRODUCTION by FRANÇOIS MAURIAC

PAUL ELEK
THIRTY-EIGHT HATTON GARDEN
LONDON

copyright by
PAUL ELEK PUBLISHERS LTD.
37-38 Hatton Garden, London, E.C.1.

printed by
CHAS. PEARSON & SON, LTD.
53-55 Mansell Street, London, E.1.

typography and layout by
PETER RAY, M.S.I.A.

translated by
DILYS OWEN

CATALOGUE NUMBER 164/9
1 9 4 7

CONTENTS

François Mauriac

FOREWORD

Jacques Boell is one of those enthusiasts who insist that we shall share their passion, even though he pretends to be writing only for himself.

A love of mountaineering, in a man, is more than anything the child in him which refuses to die. He still wants to play, to forget life in a clean game, a game which has nothing in common with war, which does not set man against man, a game without brutality, without violence, without hatred—a game which is a passion. For it is a question of conquering, not a living being, but Nature herself. It is a question of possessing the earth, the sky, the sunshine, but possessing them almost alone, and of this possession being a victory, the fruit of immense effort.

In the mountains there often comes a time, at least I have found it so, when you wish you had never started, when you curse yourself, but a single minute pays for all, and it is this minute you remember. Nature lends herself to all men, but she gives herself only to a few. That is the lesson of this salutary book. It offers young people what seems a purely physical delight, but one which touches the soul. Above a certain height it is impossible to nourish evil thoughts; there are some thoughts which cannot flourish except in the lowlands. Even as the body mounts, so the soul transcends itself; on the peaks a coarse creature becomes less coarse, and a noble being may sometimes meet God.

The risks and perils faced together, the mutual help necessary every instant, those cordées which unite more than bodies—it is plain to see how the mountains can educate a man. And when the summit is finally conquered, there is that repose beneath the eye of God, that emotion shared in silence, which a single word would shatter. A bond unites those who have shared this joy. When they return to " the huge plain where the barbarians encamp," no politics can divide them. For the lovers of the mountains are not jealous one of another; theirs is a love which brings unity.

Thanks, then, to Jacques Boell for introducing us to all the secrets of his beloved massif, and for having believed us worthy of it.

Chapter One

REMINISCENCES

Have you ever, on some lovely summer's day, stretched yourself out on the grass and dreamily watched the clouds' celestial cruising ? Across the great spaces of the open sky move the fleecy caravels, slow and majestic, and as they go, a frenzied crew is forever at work in their rigging ; up goes jib or topsail, down comes foresail or spanker. The cloud which is now at the zenith you would find impossible to describe as you first saw it on the horizon a little while before; your sole remaining impression is confused, upset by the successive changes.

In the same way, when I take refuge, far from present-day cares, in the mist of my alpine memories, despite my efforts to recall the happy moments which have sailed the seas of my past, I find moving through the shadows of time only vague silhouettes, blurred and already falsified by the dreams which have become mingled with them. A few touches alone stand out in this evocation ; they form the web—all else is embroidery and restoration.

For the three climbs I intend to describe, I have had to go back eleven years, to that dim yesterday where memories of what have been melt into memories of what might have been, as sea and sky melt together on the horizon. So I shall not attempt to tell these stories at length, but simply to record the few clear impressions which remain with me.

1. The North Peak of the Cavales (11.037 feet) by the western arête

September 18th, 1933.

(To this magnificent granite belvedere, straddling the valleys of Les Etançons and Les Cavales, there were up until 1933 only two ways of access, the easy southern and eastern arêtes. But in that year, three of my friends, Maurice, Georges and Henri Berthet, accompanied by the guide Henri Turc, opened a splendid new pure rock itinerary, the western arête. Our party made the second ascent shortly afterwards. Since then, the course has become classic; today it has probably been done more than a couple of hundred times. It forms a climb quite as interesting as that of the Aiguille Dibona du Soreiller, but unfolds in a more " high-mountain " setting).

Low and sheltered, huddled against some huge rocks, dark, damp, dirty and dilapidated, such was the Chatelleret refuge; but the setting redeemed all the discomforts. There between La Meije and Les Ecrins you cannot help but hear the heartbeat of our Oisans, and each separate peak which hemmed it in had its own particular happy recollection for us. Besides, you somehow felt in that old cabin the shades of the conquerors of the massif, who used it at a time when there were no others and every summit still held all its mystery.

Now, at the end of the season, the refuge had been abandoned to its solitude; already it smelt deserted.

The night fell quickly, and with it came a treacherous fog; we shut the door in its face like the nuisance it was. Soon a heavy slumber took possession of the Chatelleret; the nocturnal silence was broken only by a hundred mysterious little sounds and four quiet co-mingling breaths.

In a cloud-walled prison, the party climbed the Cavales footpath; the thick sodden air deadened all noise, even as it absorbed the light and altered the appearance of everything. We had run straight into it when we emerged from the cabin shortly before; the beggar had been waiting for us all night like a watchdog outside the closed door. So we had hung about a bit to see what the weather would do, but at

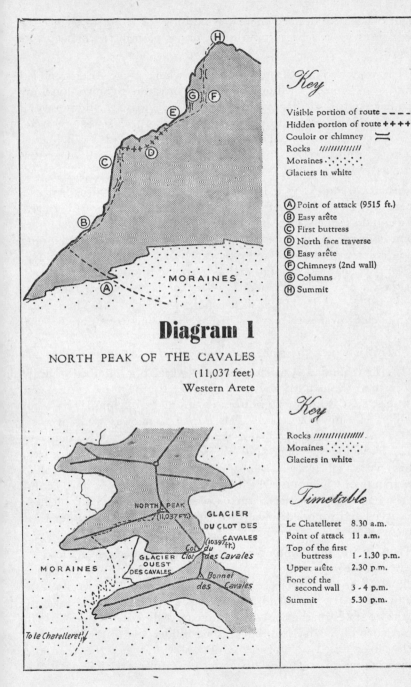

Key

Visible portion of route - - - -
Hidden portion of route + + + +
Couloir or chimney ⫤
Rocks ///////////////
Moraines ∴∴∴∴
Glaciers in white

Ⓐ Point of attack (9515 ft.)
Ⓑ Easy arête
Ⓒ First buttress
Ⓓ North face traverse
Ⓔ Easy arête
Ⓕ Chimneys (2nd wall)
Ⓖ Columns
Ⓗ Summit

Diagram I

NORTH PEAK OF THE CAVALES
(11,037 feet)
Western Arete

MORAINES

NORTH PEAK (11,037 FT.)
GLACIER DU CLOT DES CAVALES (10397 ft.)
Col du Clot des Cavales
GLACIER OUEST DES CAVALES
MORAINES
Bonnet des Cavales
To le Chatelleret

Key

Rocks ///////////////
Moraines ∴∴∴∴
Glaciers in white

Timetable

Le Chatelleret	8.30 a.m.
Point of attack	11 a.m.
Top of the first buttress	1 - 1.30 p.m.
Upper arête	2.30 p.m.
Foot of the second wall	3 - 4 p.m.
Summit	5.30 p.m.

eight o'clock we decided there was nothing for it but to chance the very short approach; autumn often has a pleasant surprise up its sleeve.

The track wound through meadows where foggy tears trembled from every stem; travelling blind, I told my three companions, my brother André, the camera man Ichac, and Plossu the humorist, all the vicissitudes of a previous attempt on the peak's western arête. We soon reached the moraine where the path faded out. At a guess, it would be best to steer a northerly course until we hit the spur we meant to climb.

Just then, almost as if it had been promised, the mist began to break up; great blue rents appeared along the neighbouring ridges. We could see the surface of it close by, quivering and whirling under some compulsion imperceptible to us; the whole mass was thinning and dissipating, and soon there remained of it nothing but a plume of vapour, light as a Chopin melody, twisted about the North Peak. At the far end of Les Etançons, where the last waves of the sea of cloud still rolled, La Meije, all streaming with light, lifted her proud granite cliff towards the sky. The day was going to be pure delight.

" This is where the real trouble starts."

The first hundred yards of the spur were soon climbed—hardly a breather. I had led my party briskly to the foot of the first buttress, split from top to bottom by a long gash, chimney to begin with, then simply a crack. This corner-stone was built of rock whose very aspect gripped you, like the glance of some women; tall slabs of yellowish rough-grained protogine, with rounded edges, which were a gift from heaven to mountaineering maniacs. (Unlike the granite of Chamonix, which is hard, sharp, geometric and painful to the hands, that of the Oisans is pleasant to the touch, polished, all curved and rounded; it calls for suppleness and grip rather than violent effort).

Halfway up, my climbing-partner, Ichac, claimed the honour of leading the attack on the rest of the lower wall. I agreed more than willingly, knowing from previous experience how little to my taste the fissure was. My friend, having placed a piton, battled savagely in the confines of the rock; he climbed slowly but relentlessly. In the silence his hoarse breathing rasped louder and louder, for every inch gained called for furious effort; now and then he muttered something which might have been either prayer or curse.

With the usual detachment of seconds, I belayed him even while I was admiring the Meije group; between peaceful contemplations of the scenery I kept a watchful eye on his progress. Soon I could see nothing but his crêpe-rubber soles, but he was still struggling on. Loop by loop the rope went up after him, as though swallowed by the cleft, a gigantic mouth of rock sucking up *spaghetti à l'italienne*. But it stopped at last, and indistinct shouts from aloft told me that the pitch had been overcome. My turn, then. No more star-gazing for me.

The pitch began with a long golden slab, above which was a projecting wall; higher up, the first slid under the second. You had to climb in the angle of their two planes, barely supported by the right arm and leg wedged into the fault, whilst left hand and foot anxiously felt the surface in vain search of holds to assist you. As a last refinement, the cleft rose in arcs; each time you made a painful end of one, another confronted you.

Still, being second over such a pitch was child's play; all danger was removed by the stout rope stretching ahead, limp or taut according to the help you needed. Being leader was something else again. No doubt that, or something very like it, was what was in his mind when I joined Ichac on a brown shelf, only to find him at grips with an insuperable nausea as the result of his violent efforts.

But new obstacles drew us on up the rocky path we had chosen.

Before starting on an oblique traverse across a steep face of broken rock, turned northwards to the shade, the two cordées held a council of war as to the best route to follow. Going on the advice of my friend Berthet, who had first succeeded in scaling the arête, I held that we must climb the frightful wall and not follow the crest to the right, where certain places looked quite impossible. Despite our justifiable dislike for a wall so black, so shadowed and so rotten, it had to be done, not without sighs of regret for the fine tawny rock and warm sunshine we were leaving.

Of this difficult and exposed passage, several hundred yards in height, I have only a vague and blurred recollection, but it is most certainly a bad one, such as you retain of a nightmare, a visit to the dentist, or a failed examination. A series of chimneys inclined at an angle of 45 degrees towards the void, with few and fragile holds, blazed a trail as unattractive as it was dangerous. We used a lot of pitons, but they seemed far too unsteady to save the cordées, in the event of a fall, from hurtling down on to the moraines nearly a thousand feet sheer below.

André led the way calmly and surely from chimney to chimney, but beneath his apparent indifference and ours was a gnawing discomfort we would none of us admit; the insecurity of the rock, the void clinging to us like a devil-fish, the impossibility of breaking a fall, all wrung our nerves for an interminable hour. It was with very real relief that we saw each rope's-length bring us nearer to the sun-splashed terminal ridge. A few yards more, and we tore ourselves away from the sinister black wall to plunge into the bath of light which awaited us on the crest.

(Later we discovered that our information had been incorrect, and now all cordées follow the arête itself. The climb is much finer, since it avoids the particularly exposed and dangerous traverse across the north face).

The party made its way along the crest of the ridge—an enormous Renaissance roof between two gable-ends. Unhurriedly we followed every tiny contour of this jetty battered by warm waves of light; after more than an hour of nervous tension, the aerial but easy footbridge stretched above the abyss was a great relaxation. The up-thrusting granite, having exhausted the strength of its first bound, seemed to be gathering itself together to push up the summit another 600 feet against the limpid sky.

The battle was not yet over; there was still an exciting fight to come. The second wall awaited us at the end of the path, and its air was frankly not welcoming. Before accosting this forbidding personage, we decided to recruit our strength and consider what turn the conversation should take; comfortably installed on a shelf, we studied the problem with the aid of all the good things motherly love had put into our haversacks.

From our position, the face to be climbed presented two possible alternatives; where it joined the arête, a series of short parallel cracks, a regular cluster of Doric columns, or on the right, several chimneys which overlooked the west Combe des Cavales, and appeared to join the other route higher up. According to my recollection, the first conquerors had climbed the columns and we could not do better than follow suit. But whether they chose the wrong point of attack, or whether their hearts were not really in it, the André-Plossu team could not get to the top, so Ichac and I, in face of this unusual marking-time and the advanced hour, decided to have a shot meanwhile at the couloirs.

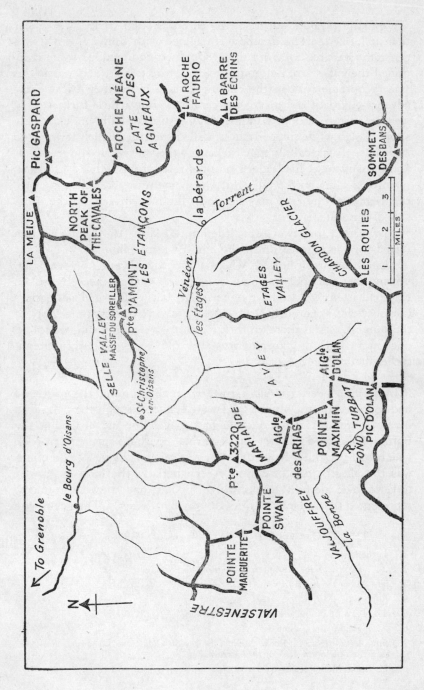

We had a pleasant surprise; the climb, though tricky, was easier than it looked. The depths were coated with thin ice, but it was generally possible to avoid this. Our two companions soon abandoned their ill-starred attempt and followed our cordée, passing us at a favourable fork in the chimney; once more they became the advance-guard of our zigzagging caravan. But a little further on, a steeper passage stopped them; André tussled with an extremely slippery slab while his partner straddled the ridge which terminated against it. Very calmly they exchanged their respective impressions, and Plossu, to set his leader's mind at rest, propounded a Cartesian plan for dealing with a fall: " If you come unstuck, yell out ' left ' or ' right ', as the case may be, and I'll chuck myself off the other side of the arête."

My brother, however, was little impressed by the idea; he preferred for his part to finish the climb without falling.

More couloirs followed, where the cordées went up feverishly, sensing that the goal was now quite near. Slabs, screes, a broken ridge, all attempted to delay our passage, but we brushed aside these last obstacles ; charging, heads-down, we took possession eagerly of the summit. And there, in the gold of the westering sun, we found once more, faithfully keeping tryst, our old, yet ever-youthful friend, the exaltation of the peak.

By leaning over, I could retrace from the summit the route we had followed up the spur, as if I were leafing through the parts of a lovely symphony the mountain had played for us. Right at the bottom I glimpsed the first buttress; this superb up-springing of rock which had provided from the start the general theme of the climb was the allegro, full of sonority. Higher up, the long shadowed traverse over decayed rock, where anxiety had drawn our faces, represented the andante with its gloomy harmonies. Then came the

THE PHOTOGRAPHS ON THE FOLLOWING PAGES

relaxation, the gay sunny walk along the crenellated wall; the notes rose up, became airy, dancing, light as flutings of joy—like a scherzo. But the fun was soon over; the cliff reared itself again. Chimneys, slabs, clefts came in quick succession, mingled and overrode one another; the brass burst into the finale, the violin-bows fluttered, and the peak struck the ultimate chord.

It was five o'clock. The sinking sun touched the wild ridge running from Le Pavé to the Cavales, whose turrets looked like twisting flames suddenly congealed in their infernal dance. Across the tragic shell of the Col du Diable the shadow of La Grande Ruine stretched ever longer.

The four of us were as one in the fullness of our happiness. There is no other earthly joy so pure and ethereal as that to be found in the sanctuary of the peaks, where you may soak it up to the point of drunkenness. No doubt this joy is so intense and complete because it transports at one and the same time the body, pleasantly tired by exercise, and the soul, exalted by the successful struggle and the beauty of the setting. Besides, at the extreme limit of these capes which push out into the ocean of the sky, you are already halfway to Paradise.

2. Crossing from Pointe Maximin (10,837 feet) to l'Aiguille d'Olan (11,060 feet) by the arête

July 16th, 1933.

These two peaks are situated on the chain which separates the upper valley of the Bonne from that of the Lavey, between Les Arias and the Pic d'Olan. The Aiguille d'Olan is easily reached from Fond Turbat; Pointe Maximin, on the other hand, had received few visits before ours.

For hours the rain had been beating steadily and furiously against the cabin roof; a damp cold creeping into the refuge nibbled you between the shoulder-blades. Through the gathering dusk beyond the dull window-panes we could see an endless march-past of vast regiments of fog, fleeing before that worst of all omens, a west wind

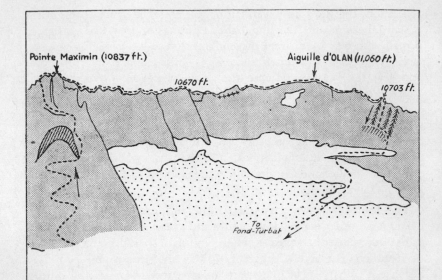

Diagram 2

THE POINTE MAXIMIN— AIGUILLE d'OLAN ARETE

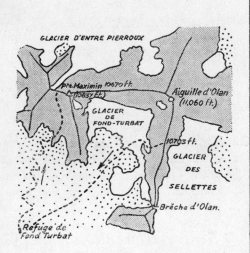

Key

Route _ _ _ _ _ _ _ _
Rocks //////////////
Moraines ·.·.·.·.·.·.·.
Arêtes ≫≫≫≫≫≫≫≫≫
Glaciers in white

Timetable

Refuge   5 a.m.
Pointe Maximin 9 - 10.30 a.m.
Aiguille d'Olan 2 - 2.30 p.m.
Refuge   5.30 p.m.

sweeping up the valley. Now and again amidst the soft patter of
the rain came the clear note of a drop of water falling into an empty
tin-can, already three parts full.

A rainy day at Fond Turbat, far from the madding crowd, is at
the same time a retreat right out of this world, and a stiff trial of
patience for four chaps more inclined for action than meditation.

My friends, Alain Le Ray and Guy Labour, had come up to attempt
the immense inhuman west wall of the Pic d'Olan, still virgin and
the object of many unfulfilled desires. (Alain said of it: "After a
climb like that, it wouldn't matter if you made a complete mess of
your life. You could even do something thoroughly stupid, like
getting married.") My brother André and I were a bit scared of a
trip on that scale; our more modest but quite attractive project was
the first crossing from Pointe Maximin to the Aiguille d'Olan, and
the poor weather conditions had compelled our comrades to throw
in their lot with ours.

When we arrived the day before, there were several mountaineers
at the refuge, but they had gone down that morning, completely
discouraged, so we had the Fond Turbat cabin to ourselves. Fond
Turbat ! I know of no other easily accessible retreat where you feel
so intensely the tragic grandeur of the mountains, the crushing power
of nature, and the harmony of the divine creation.

Taking advantage of a break in the clouds, the party, to kill time
and see what the prospects were, made a reconnaissance as far as the
first tier of the savage two-headed giant who is unquestioned king of
those regions, the Pic d'Olan. But a fresh attack by the rain in
heavy squalls drove us back to the refuge we had left two hours previously. To warm us up on our return, we prepared a roaring fire
and some scalding concentrated soup, which "tastes of fluffed
climbs," according to Alain, who was reminded by this hasty
cookery of his early, and not always fortunate, days in the mountains.

Aided and abetted by the fog, night made an early invasion of the
cabin; gossiping by the trembling light of a candle, we laid plans
without much conviction, while the rain whispered untiringly outside.
So there was nothing for it but to go to bed, offer up little prayers
to the god of climbers for a clear day tomorrow, and fall asleep—to
dream of a sky perpetually blue.

While it did not entirely answer our prayers, Providence had
certainly listened to them with one ear. The dawn was actually not
too disheartening, so we decided to try our luck. The party would

simply have to be sensible enough not to get into difficulties if the weather became definitely threatening; in that way we could be sure of nothing worse than a thorough drenching, a risk we were all perfectly willing to take.

In the cold light of dawn, we started up the long monotonous slopes, first of short rain-sodden grass, then earth, freshly stripped of its snowy robes and now sprinkled with delicate anemones, and finally interminable screes, like crumbs from the feast which awaited us. Long bands of cloud came and went, rubbing across the face of the Pic d'Olan—soft towels for its morning wash.

Each of us climbed as he fancied, and we were soon high up; Fond Turbat already looked far away, as though the earth had sucked it down, but our path was still easy enough. I can remember a colossal porch of rock, like a cyclopean eye, which watched us mounting towards it; we made a wide detour to avoid this impasse, and found above it an endless ledge, a tremendous wrinkle on the mountain's brow. Further along, we crossed a narrow rocky couloir which seemed to split the cliff from the top downwards; we thought for a moment of taking advantage of this natural road, but tempting as it was, it was carpeted with ice, so we passed on in search of drier routes.

The party spread out over a series of steps which became progressively steeper; Alain, the last of the file, must have been still half-asleep, for he kept running into all sorts of unexpected difficulties, which made the rest of us hoot with laughter. While he was struggling away, Labour lashed his vanity unmercifully: "Well, well, old man ! And just think, if it hadn't been for the rain we were going to have a go at the west wall of l'Olan !" André proceeded to drop him the end of his rope, doing his best to hinder him as much as possible by this pseudo-helpful act.

After this incident, we thought it wisest to make up cordées, and quite as much from habit as for the sake of splitting the family risk, Alain and I joined forces for the day. It is a great moment when the ropes are fastened, knots adjusted, and without any idea of setbacks in your mind you tackle the first pitches of a cliff, saying, "Let's go !"

The crest could hardly be far off. Thin veils of mist swirled above it, then round the caravan; through them the rocks on either hand seemed by turn very near and very distant. Several beautiful slabs still retained a lukewarm reminder of the pale morning sunshine, which they passed on to our caressing fingers; climbing them was doubly agreeable.

Soon we were hoisting ourselves on to the ridge, only to be met and buffeted by a strong cold wind which was sweeping the northern slope. Through a rift we could see, far down, the Entre-Pierroux glacier, and in the distance Les Arias all cloaked in cloud. Ten minutes later we reached Pointe Maximin, white with hoar-frost in its cotton wool wrappings; the first and easiest part of our trip was over.

"Honestly, this thick stuff will get my goat in a minute!"

Settled several yards below the level of the peak, on the southern side well out of the wintry blast, we were prepared for a long siege.

The traverse and conquest of the tremendous ridge which stretched between Pointe Maximin and the Aiguille d'Olan involved something more than an easy stroll; several first-class cordées had already failed in the attempt. As usual, there was a minimum of information to be had about it; all we knew was that the impracticable north slope towered up almost vertically over sixteen hundred feet from the Entre-Pierroux glacier, while the south wall fell a mere eight or nine hundred feet to the Fond Turbat glaciers—a wall much less steep than its opposite number, but which had never to our knowledge been climbed. Since the only ways off this long ridge were at either end, there was no escape if bad weather overtook you halfway.

For nearly ninety minutes we had been waiting for the fog to spread its wings and take off, but it hung about obstinately, and our patience was running short. Somebody even went so far as to talk of raising the siege and going back the way we had come, but someone else—it must have been Alain—was indignant over such lack of sticking-power and voted for a longer wait.

And while we were discussing it, the impossible happened; a fierce norther snatched at our misty shroud and whipped it away. Up from the depths of the mass, all a-quiver under the conflicting currents, swam our ridge, unsubstantial, coated with rime, sprung straight out of a fairy-tale. The fog beat against its flanks in long rollers; ebbing, they left the white cliffs fringed with foam like reefs. From the gulf of Fond Turbat, rippling with cross-waves, emerged the Pic d'Olan, stern as some Nordic isle; on its fascinating virgin wall, all glazed with ice, Alain and Labour tried to make out the route they would have attempted to follow had the weather been favourable.

High in the sky there still remained a thin film of cloud, but a little goodwill on the part of the sun, and our hopes, might dissolve it. Anyhow, not wanting to believe that the clear-up, like some conversions, might be only temporary, we threw ourselves into the adventure with one accord.

Through the greyness another tower came towards us, blurred and spectral, in appearance very like all the ones before and yet quite different. There are resemblances between rocks as there are between faces; a certain similarity, though each of them has its own personality.

It was more than three hours since we had embarked hopefully on this interminable saw-toothed ridge, and we had been on the move the whole time; nevertheless the cordées, lost between earth and sky, so submerged in clouds that they could not see a single landmark, had the impression they were standing still. What had happened was that the fickle sky, too easily cleared, had lost no time in over-casting again the moment we abandoned Pointe Maximin to its solitude. Like a flood-tide, the whirling mists had risen all along the cliffs till they drowned the narrow isthmus flung between the two peaks, and from the prison which thus closed about us we could see nothing but a scrap of washed-out blue sky, wavering an instant through the clouds; after which we had worked our way for hours across the ghostly crest in a sort of gloomy clarity, a peculiar cross between day and night.

Unceasingly from the fog there emerged one after another the countless warriors, helmets and breastplates rime-edged, with which the arête sought to oppose our passage. Each time our cordées seized them with benumbed fingers and overthrew them, clambering past on one side or the other, but while still breathless the victors would see the next mist-begotten soldier looming up, and the battle would start all over again. Towers, steeples, projections, spires and campaniles had filed past, a slow and monotonous white squadron swallowed by the fog as soon as they were vanquished.

Often the clouds were so dense that I could not see the second cordée, which was nevertheless not far away; sometimes even my companion was invisible to me and the rope, like a long umbilical cord joining us together, lost itself in the mist. Since the wind drowned all sounds and cries, I had the feeling that I was indulging in solitary mountaineering.

Now and then certain configurations of the ground made us think we were nearing our goal, but some half-seen hanging névé turned out to be only a caricature of the one clinging to the Aiguille d'Olan, and the arête went on, throwing against us untiringly its faceless, numberless defenders. More rocks, more mist, more silver thaw; there was no longer anything on earth for us but these three elements, sometimes in succession, sometimes associated. Mist, rock, ice; we might have been in Spitzbergen or Victoria Land.

How inhuman this planet would be if it consisted of nothing but mountains, if there were no sea, no rivers, no woods and flowers and everything that is life, that mysterious and ephemeral reflection of God. Without them, without it, I must admit—I, who none the less extol the chaos of the peaks——that the most magnificent dawns would illuminate only a desolate earth.

In the end our alpine instinct did not play us false despite the heavy clouds. A spectral arête vanishing in the mist to the north-east recalled at once to Alain and myself a memory scarcely a year old; it was the route we had taken from La Lavey to the Aiguille d'Olan on a radiant day in July, 1932. So the peak could hardly be far away, and in ten minutes we were at the big cairn which still watched over its solitude.

A return visit to a known summit is like meeting an old friend. You say to yourself, " It hasn't changed," without being certain of reciprocity, and memories come up from the depths of your mind, things like " When I was climbing that chimney", or " Do you remember how cold it was on this arête ? " and even, " How delighted we were to get to the cairn". It is a pleasant thought that bits of the past cling like that to the countryside, all ready to be found by those who know where to look for them.

So our long trip, close against the sky, finished without incident, and unhappily without a glimpse of the view either. Nowhere, even in the places coated with a silver thaw, had we encountered nerve-racking difficulties, but looking back today I can't help thinking what we might have suffered if a real storm had hit us, or one of us had been injured halfway across the arête and had had to be carried.

In spite of the miserable weather and the fact that we were perished with cold, we stayed a long half-hour on the peak, battered by freezing winds; we were waiting for a sight of the beloved neigh-bouring summits, hoping that the heavy veil which had overhung us for more than four hours might lift if only for an instant. We had braved the mountains' frown so long that day, and now we wanted just one smile. But even that was refused us. We were forced to leave the summit without carrying off the least of those visions which are the real reason behind all passion for the heights.

Nothing remained but to descend by the usual route and pick up the beaten track again. Then suddenly we decided that it was still early and there were still new worlds to conquer; we made up our minds to prolong our cruise between earth and sky by exploring the third arête of the peak, the one which runs south towards the Brêche d'Olan. The mist certainly did not allow of any advance appreciation of the difficulties the new crossing might offer, but after the previous one nothing could frighten us. So we went blindly on again over the unknown ground, and once more the tireless chant began; mist, rocks, ice—rocks, mist, ice . . .

In the end we suddenly felt that we had had enough of the interminable ridge, enough of its anonymous and countless defenders; weary of such monotony we wanted something else besides a jagged knife-edge. Halfway between the Aiguille and the Brêche d'Olan, an attractive couloir plunging westward deep down into the fog tempted our fourfold desire for novelty.

As scout for the first cordée, I led off down the narrow bottleneck hemmed in by long black slabs; the slope became very steep, and I groped my way along at no great speed. Several times my companions gave me warning of stones they had unintentionally dislodged; it was a real strain on the nerves to hear these lumps rattling down unseen through the mist until they suddenly appeared a few yards above, hardly giving me time to get out of the way—they were like sinister black birds immediately snapped up by the stubborn, hungry fog.

All at once the slope ceased to be vertical; the couloir had brought me out above a sheer drop where it finished all slippery with thin ice. I felt it would be a good idea to get away from this hair-raising springboard overhanging the void, and looked around for a line of escape; a short but exposed traverse, followed by a tricky descent, allowed the cordées to reach a new couloir not far from the first and so avoid the uninviting wall.

It was then that the magic circle which had held us captive since the morning broke up. Little by little we came out of the fog as you come out of an anaesthetic, your mind a blank, eyes slowly taking in your surroundings. Like miners emerging dazzled from a dark drift, we passed one after another through the cloudy vault, which closed up again behind us. Below us we could now see a steep icy couloir; beyond that a hanging snow strip; lower still an untroubled glacier; and right at the bottom—we could hardly believe our eyes—the tender green of the high meadows, flecked with sunshine. It was pretty good to see living things again after our prolonged *tête-à-tête* exclusively with the mineral world and the clouds.

Another half-hour of bitter struggle on a steep icy slope, then we jumped the *rimaye*, the crevasse at the foot of the cliff, and our trip was over. " Behind us, muzzle to the ground, the glacier breathes with a cold nostril . . . "

In front of the refuge were two friends from the Groupe de Haute-Montagne, who had arrived in our absence; they watched us approach.

" Hullo, where've you been ? "

" Crossing from Pointe Maximin to the Aiguille d'Olan."

" Oh, jolly good ! "

They were real sports. Their hesitation had been barely perceptible, but all the same we had seen the shadow of disappointment in their eyes. They too had come up to Turbat to seek a little of the unknown on that long ridge which had whispered to us today, through the endless veil of mist, its humble and monotonous secret.

3. Winter Ascent of La Roche Méane
(12,176 feet)

February 19th, 1934.

La Roche Méane is the culminating point of a splendid rocky group neighbouring La Grande Ruine, the enormous spur rising between the Cavales valley and that of the Platte des Agneaux. The summits of this massif had all been climbed in winter except La Roche Méane, so we were exceedingly anxious to pull off this winter ascent.

" How much more is there of this interminable snow-slope ? I can't go another step; it's absolute agony."

Completely worn out, I was taking a few minutes rest on an out-crop of stone and saying the same thing over to myself for the hundredth time, while I gazed back unhappily the way I had come.

For nearly two hours we had been leaving our painful trail behind us. Hole had been added endlessly to hole, and heaven alone knew how many more would have to be made before we could push open the door of the Adèle Planchard refuge, for which we were already crying from the depths of our exhaustion.

We had left the Glacier des Agneaux at dusk; soon the valley was drowned in darkness and we floundered about in the gloom, but very quickly the moon, that precious poor relation, came to light our hesitating steps up the combe. On the glacier, at the foot of this immense talus, we held a conference; since the snow seemed hard and well-packed, there was no fear of avalanches, and we decided not to make the long winter detour but to climb straight up to the cabin.

Alain Le Ray was the only one who had brought his crampons, and with their aid he went swiftly up a steep couloir; the crisp sound of his easy progress lost itself little by little in the invading night. With my other companion I had chosen a less abrupt place to climb, in the hope of being able to ski up, but unfortunately the slope proved too rapid and the surface too hard for the skis to grip, and we had to take them off.

At first all went well; the snow was just right and we soon gained height. Then suddenly the picture changed; the crust which was too hard for the skis was too soft for walking, and it gave way at every step, plunging us to the knees in a powdery mess. And so our troubles began.

Each yard gained called for a constant effort of will and muscles. With dulled brains and flabby legs, the pitiful caravan went zig-zagging to and fro in vain search of better snow; we made dozens of fruitless attempts which only served to dishearten us still further, sunk as we were to the thighs and seized by the glacial cold the moment we stopped moving. As I toiled along, temples throbbing with the exertion, a tune from " Scheherazade " kept hammering relentlessly at my memory over and over again; it was like a stray dog that refuses to leave you alone.

Now and then Maurice " spelled " me in the lead, but the second's plight was really little better than that of the man who was breaking trail, for the packed snow gave way again as you trod on it, so that

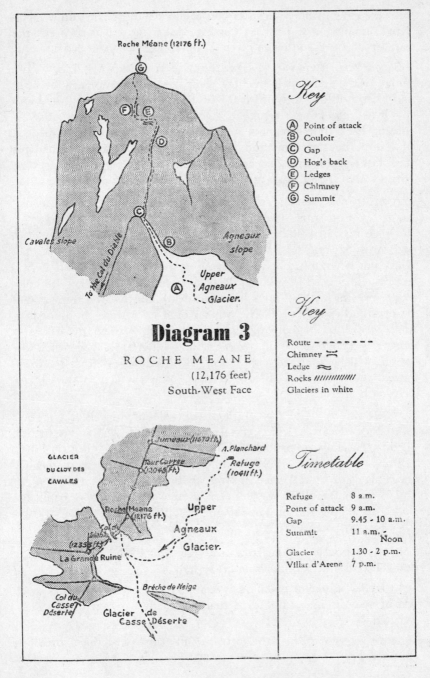

Key

- Ⓐ Point of attack
- Ⓑ Couloir
- Ⓒ Gap
- Ⓓ Hog's back
- Ⓔ Ledges
- Ⓕ Chimney
- Ⓖ Summit

Diagram 3

ROCHE MEANE
(12,176 feet)
South-West Face

Key

Route - - - - - - -
Chimney ⋛
Ledge ≈
Rocks ///////////
Glaciers in white

Timetable

Refuge	8 a.m.
Point of attack	9 a.m.
Gap	9.45 - 10 a.m.
Summit	11 a.m. - Noon
Glacier	1.30 - 2 p.m.
Villar d'Arene	7 p.m.

we were caught in a vicious circle; each cave-in of the snow aggravated our fatigue and through awkwardness caused us to break the hard crust more and more often.

To make matters worse, I got the disastrous idea of taking a cola tablet for the first time in my life to help combat my mortal weariness, and I had not long to wait for the result; in a few minutes I had lost my little remaining strength . . . I thought more than once of turning back, but somehow in spite of everything I still hoped to find some decent snow, and besides, there was Alain; we had no means of warning him, and he might spend the whole night searching for us. No, I had made my bed, and I must lie on it.

It got so that, starting off after one of our frequent pauses, I would fix my eyes on some point short of which I forbade myself to stop, but panting desperately for breath be unable to do more than half without collapsing like a worn-out beast. Sometimes a step appeared solid, but when you put your weight on it, it gave abruptly. Then, exhausted, you fell headlong, all of a piece, face down on the cold slope, praying with all your heart for death, so that the thing could be over and done with. The other would encourage the poor lost soul, in sad and unconvincing tones, to pick himself up, and the staggering progress would begin again, a long Calvary beneath the moon, which cast across the snow the blackness of our shadows bowed under the burden of our skis. Was there no Cyrenian to help us bear our cross?

The clear cold sky was studded with splendid jewels; the moonlight flooded certain cliffs, certain glaciers, while the arêtes in the shadow stood up fantastically against the starry dome. But we cared nothing for all that. Tonight only one thing mattered—to get to the refuge. If by the grace of God we did reach it, it was journey's end as far as the climb was concerned anyway, since there could be no possible question of going a single step further next day.

"And they call this sport!"

In my aching head the same notes of Rimsky were still beating, going round and round like a crazy mill.

"Well," as Alain maliciously claimed later on, "I suppose it was at some moment like that, that you made up your mind to get married."

In other words, as an antidote for our particular form of drunkenness!

Finally, when we were practically at our last gasp, we heard, quite close at hand, the cheerful voice of our companion, who had arrived at the cabin a long time before; he was standing calling to us from the lighted rectangle of the doorway.

I had never quite realised before how much the word " refuge " meant; it represented arms spread wide to our distress, warmth for our cold, rest for our weariness—a sort of deliverance. Dazed with fatigue, Maurice and I reeled into the cabin and dropped in our tracks, completely incapable of answering Alain's questions. In the silence, broken only by the sizzling of the stove, I could hear the blood beating furiously in my breast and temples, while bells rang endlessly in my wretched brain. I must have stayed foundered for some minutes in this state of blankness, which is probably very like death, when I felt Alain's hand on my shoulder.

" Come on, pal. The soup's hot and you'll feel better after it. Tomorrow we'll make a great climb, see if we don't, and you'll soon forget all about this."

" A great climb." The words acted like a charm. I began to feel my longing coming back irresistibly from the depths whither I had consigned it forever; to scale La Roche Méane—provided that by tomorrow I had recovered my strength.

I found Maurice already at the table; he looked played out, but I knew that at heart he felt as I did.

In the rays of the sun, still low in the east, the hard snow-crystals were iridescent with a thousand fires, the rocky islets emerging from the glacier projected vast shadows, and the snowclad arêtes flirted with the light, telling all the foolish stories the wind had carved on them. We were nearing the Col du Diable, a notch of blue sky in the tawny rock; up to then our progress had been easy enough, a useful limbering-up for muscles stiffened by our last night's exertions.

To my great satisfaction, I felt in good physical trim; Berthet, however, had made a less complete recovery, and this morning he had wanted to give up the trip for fear of being a burden to us. We had had quite a job to overcome his scruples. Now that after the terrible trials of his life's end he is no more than a shade among shades, it makes me very happy to think that by my insistence I helped that day to give him one of the great joys of his existence.

We roped up before starting on the climb proper; Alain as usual took the lead, without the slightest need for discussion. When we are together I never aspire to anything more than being his faithful second. The rope, tangible symbol of our mutual affection, has united us so many times; I only hope it may bind us together as often in the future as it has in the past, and that we both still have many wonderful days to come in the mountains.

The south slope of La Roche Méane which we intended to climb was in splendid condition, dry and clean-swept as though it were the height of summer. A long series of fine days had given the mountain a welcoming smile. Looking round as far as the eye could see at all the valleys, all the immaculate peaks softened by a bluish haze, you could not help feeling that you were in some immaterial world where everything was beauty and purity.

The itinerary advocated by the guide-books follows the couloirs in the shadow of the west slope, but Alain knew of a fine, direct, though extremely unorthodox route to our objective; the rocky south-west arête, which we should strike about one third of the way up. We felt that our luck was in today and we could not possibly fail.

The cordée, having crossed without any difficulty some snowy slopes which must have been full of yawning crevasses in summer, clambered lightly up a narrow couloir towards the desired spur. Alain ploughed hard, but with tremendous vigour, through the thick snow which is only to be found on the heights, and presently we were all standing in the smooth notch of an opening at the mouth of our couloir. From there to the summit a lovely ridge of brown rock hung delicately poised between the Cavales abyss and the frightful Couloir du Diable.

Action is very calming to nerves which have been stretched by long awaiting it, and so the minutes we spent on this long flight of stone which bore us gently up towards the sky were filled with delight. When I think of it, even after a lapse of ten years, I can still feel on my fingers the pleasant warmth radiating from the rocks (though I hardly dare write it of a winter climb) and the fresh breeze blowing in my face; the marvellous landscape I can never forget.

My small remaining fatigue had vanished the moment I first touched the rock; I felt like another being, all cleansed of the weariness of life. The arête played with the cordée as a wave plays with a cork, tossing it from one flank to the other or lifting it on the very crest, till at last it humped itself up and deposited its burden at the foot of the final wall.

Alain brought us all up beside him before tackling the problem, then set off on a traverse towards the Cavales side, where he studied

a chimney before starting calmly up it and disappearing. The rope
went up behind him, slowly at first, then faster, then very fast, and
we heard a triumphant shout :

" Summit ! "

An hour later, near the cairn, we were still savouring the pleasure
of intimacy with this peak, so far from all human life. Everywhere
we looked there was nothing but whiteness on whiteness, blue
shadows in the valleys and on the cliffs, and overhead, a sky so clear
and limpid it seemed no cloud could ever veil it. An infinite peace
and mellowness had fallen on us; such is the great appeasement
which comes from the friendship of a mountain.

The thought had often crossed my mind in town on a glorious
winter day : '' What wouldn't I give to be up in the Oisans now ! ''

Well, here I was, and on what a peak ! One of the last to be
scaled in winter, so all my cherished dreams came true in one fell
swoop. Close by, La Tour Carrée lifted its tall cliff to the sun's
caresses; I could plainly see the route I had followed up the wall
on my first mountaineering campaign without a guide. I could
recall every detail of it as clearly as though it had been yesterday
instead of five years before.

While the animal in us, basking in the warmth, was greedily
enjoying the assuaging of its hunger and fatigue, the soul was busy
gathering from the beauty spread before us that ethereal joy which
gives a meaning to our passion and makes us, for the moment, nearly
pure spirit. There is a violent contrast between the lofty ideals
inspired by the mountains and the base material necessities they also
impose.

At the bottom of the last pitch we unfastened the rope and put on
our skis, which had been waiting for us as good as gold, then off we
went on the long white run over two thousand yards of ups and
downs, along the extreme end of the Glacier des Agneaux, past the
foot of the tragic cliffs of the Tête de Charrière and the Roche
d'Alvau, realm of eternal solitude. As I went sweeping across the
ridges and down into the combes, full of satisfaction at ' bringing
home the bacon,' up from the depths of my being came a familiar
tune. The music of " Scheherazade " was still pursuing me with
its strange enchantment, but today, instead of yesterday's frenzied
rhythm, it was a sort of vibrant alleluia whose notes came welling
up like fresh spring water.

Chapter Two

THE NORTH FACE OF LES ARIAS

Les Arias (11,149 feet) are situated on the long arête running from the Pic d'Olan to La Muzelle. They dominate the valleys of the Mariande, the Lavey and Fond Turbat. The normal route takes the cliff on the south face, towards Fond Turbat.

July 11th, 1937. It was five o'clock in the morning.

A radiant dawn tinted the peaks, the arêtes stood clear-cut against a crystal sky, trailing mists filled the valley-depths, and an icy breath of wind swept the mountains. It was the Mariande valley, a corner of the Oisans as appealing as any in its vast loneliness, its towering cliffs and the variety of its meadow flowers.

Two mountaineers were crossing the screes, coming from the Alpe du Pin, where they had spent the night. They had left Grenoble the previous afternoon and gone up heavily laden to the chalet from Saint-Christophe; a gentle dusk had fallen while they sat among the flowering rhododendrons swapping stories of their experiences in the mountains.

THE PHOTOGRAPHS ON THE FOLLOWING PAGES

9. From left to right: Les Arias (north slope) and the Pointes du Grand Vallon, with the Lauranoure Lake in the foreground. (From an oil painting by Mme. Boell.)
10. The snow-slope above the rimaye on Les Arias
11. The depths of Valsenestre. From left to right: Pointes Gaillard, Henriette, Marguerite and Royer
12. The summit
13. Rock climb on Pointe Swan
14. Pointe Swan from Pointe Royer. The dotted line shows the route up the west slope
15. The Bonnepierre face of Les Ecrins
16. Cloud effect

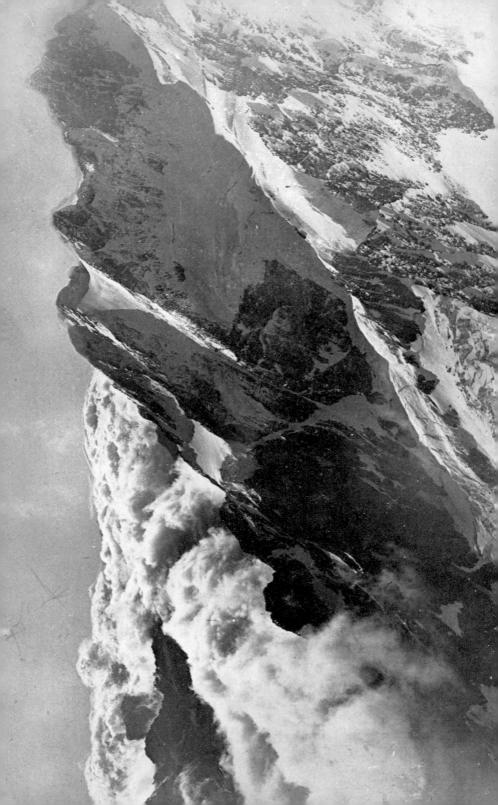

This morning they had talked over their project—to climb the north face of Les Arias. They knew little about it beyond the fact that it had been done a dozen years previously by Pierre Dalloz, and somewhat later by Jean Escarra; they had certainly read accounts of these two expeditions at the time, but now their recollections of them were rather vague. Still, in some ways that was an advantage; theirs would be almost the joy of the discoverer.

This was a trip that one of them had been wanting to make for over three years. Time and time again he had looked at the cliff from the neighbouring summits and thought, "I simply must do that," as though the desire created an imperative obligation to make the climb. Then the months would go by, otherwise occupied, but the temptation of the mountain, with the name as sweet and rough as itself, still persisted. And so at last this year he had decided to try his luck, and invited his young companion to provide both moral and physical support.

They left the moraines and tackled the glacier, which was protected by a plinth of slabs. The sunlight was beginning to flood the cliff they sought, throwing it into relief; they could not take their eyes off this wall whose secret they wished so ardently to possess. They put on crampons and continued their monotonous tramp, spikes rasping over the curdled ice; soon both were wrapped in their thoughts, lulled by the even rhythm of their steps.

The elder of the two looked at the heights about him with a gaze at once loving and sad. All too brief were the moments of joy he could live in the mountains he adored; too many things stood in the way of his passion for climbing, which there was no denying took the best that was in him. He had a feeling that the hours he might still devote to it were numbered: the struggle for existence, the strain of his work, the weight of years, the duties and joys of a family, the fear of death—not for himself but for those left behind—were all obstacles to the enthusiastic practice of mountaineering. The road he might still travel was unhappily a great deal shorter than that already covered.

They reached the fallen séracs; the ice-axe came into play, and action drove away gloomy thoughts. The rope stretched out between the two friends, step after step was cut, the crampons grated.

The younger of the pair climbed swiftly up the blazed trail to rejoin his leader. The mountains were sheer delight to him; no bitterness for the past touched his ardent youth. For him every cliff

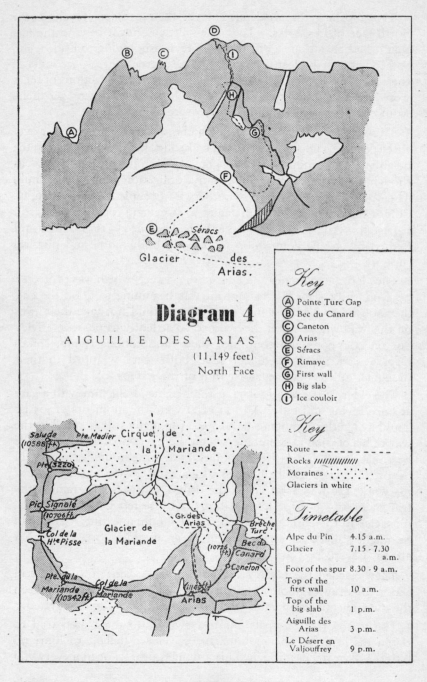

Diagram 4

AIGUILLE DES ARIAS

(11,149 feet)

North Face

Key

- Ⓐ Pointe Turc Gap
- Ⓑ Bec du Canard
- Ⓒ Caneton
- Ⓓ Arias
- Ⓔ Séracs
- Ⓕ Rimaye
- Ⓖ First wall
- Ⓗ Big slab
- Ⓘ Ice couloir

Key

Route - - - - - - - -
Rocks //////////////
Moraines ·.·.·.·.·.·
Glaciers in white

Timetable

Alpe du Pin	4.15 a.m.
Glacier	7.15 - 7.30 a.m.
Foot of the spur	8.30 - 9 a.m.
Top of the first wall	10 a.m.
Top of the big slab	1 p.m.
Aiguille des Arias	3 p.m.
Le Désert en Valjouffrey	9 p.m.

was a challenge; he thought only of fighting his way to the top. The rope that day bound together more than two friends animated by the same love of the heights; it united yesterday's climber with tomorrow's.

The crampons clawed at the frozen snow; the slope stiffened, reared and broke off—it was the *rimaye*. Fortunately the lateness of the snow made it possible to cross the obstacle; for a moment the two companions walked the tight-rope on a thin blade of ice, then they set foot once more on the slope, and the axe went to work again carving out notches. The rope unreeled again till they came to the base of a two-thousand foot promontory, where action would make the hours pass like minutes.

They took off their crampons and began the easy climb over frost-glazed and very decayed rock. The sun was at last coming into sight above the Bec du Canard arête; they decided that a pause would be very welcome on a wide ledge dominating the rapid slope of the north-east face. Looking upwards, the usual effect of the perspective made the rest of the cliff seem short and easy, a double error of judgment which the two friends committed in spite of their knowledge of the mountains.

It became a prolonged halt on the airy terrace; the cordée, in a nice warm spot, was savouring the deep solitude of the heights. Their gaze strayed from summits to cliffs, taking rapid notes to store in their memory; corrugated snow-slopes, out of the sun, rushing down towards the *rimaye;* the valley spread out so far below that all relief had vanished; a jagged arête with rambling spires; a snowy pinnacle exquisitely lit; and overhead the intensely blue sky to which the peak lifted—the whole of the high mountains was in these few impressions. The two companions were conscious of the delight the setting gave them, of how much they were made for this fierce and ardent background. One of them, rather attracted by the idea of metempsychosis, made a vow deep in his heart to be reborn a chamois.

Presently they started to climb again. A promontory reared itself before them, and the cordée attacked it eagerly; they worked their way between the slabs by some good cracks and convenient ledges, reached the crest of the arête, straddled it, and hoisted themselves to the peak, only to meet with a big disappointment. This was only a minor summit; beyond it there was still to scale all the height of a most forbidding cliff. To the left was a colossal roof-shaped slab, well over three hundred feet high, to the right a ruinous wall of purest " north face " type, vertical, decayed, and apparently without any weak point; over the whole a rocky blackish pediment raised itself up against the sky. Obviously the thing to do was to reach the huge slab and follow it to its end; beyond that—well, beyond that they must hope for the best.

Somewhat impressed by the stern prospect, the two companions, agreeing that on this trip they had certainly had their cake first, prepared to attempt the ideal route they had picked out. To begin with it was necessary to make a short rocky descent to a snowclad shoulder, since the spur they had climbed did not join on to the cliff itself. On a steep ice-slope the younger was able to try his hand at cutting steps, the rope unwinding slowly behind him; the second followed him up and they carried on. The leader crossed the gleaming incline, which was broken by several outcrops of rock; his companion rejoined and then passed him, and from a tiny shelf tackled the immense roof-shaped slab.

The scaling of this was actually much simpler than it had appeared, the only trouble being that the rock was abominably decayed and called for extreme care. In a few bounds the chunks they dislodged reached a long slope of snow which prolonged the slab, and flew whistling towards the *rimaye* thirteen hundred feet below. It was a terrific strain on the nerves to watch these stones go hurtling down to the depths of the glacier; they emphasised only too clearly the angle of the slope and the height of the cliff.

The cordée rapidly gained altitude, but the upper part of the slab, glazed with ice across all its width, stopped them dead; somehow they must by-pass it. A careful examination showed the pair the beginnings of a chimney in the cliff which dominated them, and the younger tackled it with infinite precaution; the angle was stiff and the rock extremely decomposed. The clear note of hammer on piton rang out in the silence, followed by the sharp click of a closing karabiner, and the cordée's safety was assured.

At the top was a shoulder from which a brief descent took them back on to the big slab, close to its crest, avoiding the glazed part very nicely. And there, they found simple touching evidence of a past already twelve years old; a cairn set up by the first climbing-party. They snatched a few minutes' rest; the towering black cliffs, seamed with icy couloirs which plunged down right to the glacier, frowned on them.

But it was already late; if they meant to return to Grenoble that night the summit must be reached as soon as possible—so the ascent was resumed. There followed a long, easy, rising ledge, a succession of steps, each of which proved a disappointment, an exposed traverse above a gulf, and at last an ice-collared summit, the true one, they hoped, dominated the cordée. The left fork, leading to a gap, seemed the most likely, though the slope was extreme, and the couloir full of terribly hard-frozen snow. The younger started up, cutting steps painstakingly and testing all the rocky outcrops for holds. The elder followed his progress with an anxiety that was almost paternal.

"Take care, kid. This damned rock's all rotten. Use plenty of pitons, and if you find it's a bit too difficult or dangerous——"

But the leader was already halfway up; perched on a minute ledge he was fixing a piton, which after going in very unwillingly an inch at the most refused to penetrate further. No matter; it would be enough to serve as a foothold. The second joined him, his morale at a low ebb.

"It's getting terribly late. Don't you think we ought to turn back, seeing how careful we'll have to be on that bad rock ?"

But the younger was indignant at the mere idea of missing the summit by so little.

"Give me another quarter of an hour."

"O.K."

And on they went. There was a brief tussle with a sheet of pure ice, then some big screes led them to a very boxed-in gap giving on to the Lavey slope. The cordée stood ready for the final assault on a vertical wall fifteen or twenty feet high, followed by a less sheer slab whose height it was difficult to estimate from below.

The younger claimed the well-earned honour of leading the last lap; he abandoned rucksack and axe, studied the problem carefully and tackled it with the utmost calm. He climbed smoothly and athletically, with safety rather than style, and a few nicely co-ordinated efforts soon polished off the first part, but success gave him wings, and the slab in turn was summarily dealt with. There came a shout of delight.

René Nicolet was on the summit of Les Arias.

July, 1938.

Chapter Three

DU CÔTÉ DE LA POINTE SWAN

This peak (10,807 feet) is situated on the ridge which separates the basin of the Vénéon from that of the Lavey, between La Muzelle and L'Olan. From its summit springs a spur which divides the Upper Valbonnais en Jouffrey from Valsenestre. The peak is very little frequented; its rare visitors have all reached it by the north-east, from the Lanchâtra valley, except for one cordée which scaled its southern arête.

Because of its title, I thought at first of treating this story in the manner of Marcel Proust, but I soon gave up the idea. According to your opinion of the Master, some of you will think, '' What impudence ! '' and others, '' We've had a narrow escape ! '' That is why I shall stick to the plain and simple style which comes naturally to me.

A number of projected climbs had taken us up to Valsenestre, and I found myself seized with an ever-increasing affection for that wooded valley, that little lost corner and the mountains which encircled it. The serried forests, the dying hamlet, the flowery meadows and harsh cliffs with their jagged arêtes exhaled a disturbing charm that drew and intoxicated me, and more than anything the solitude, sweetest of companions, by whose grace I enter into possession of the kingdom of the wilderness on the heights . . .

1. First Attempt on Pointe Swan

July 7th, 1938.

Four tents stood in a circle at the edge of the Combe Oursière wood, close against the Béranger torrent. I had come up to camp in my beloved valley with a group of friends who wanted to get off the beaten track, and tomorrow they were certainly going to, for we planned on climbing one of the peaks east of La Muzelle, at the far end of the cirque. After some discussion we had decided to try the west slope of Pointe Swan, which hems in the little Coin Charnier glacier, pleasant in appearance however sinister it may be in name.

We sang sociable songs late into the night; above the spikes of the tall black firs the sky seemed to be hatching stars. We called up memories of the numerous friends who had already lost their lives in the mountains; perhaps their spirits were in the great fresh breeze which touched our faces and fled into the forest, whispering through the branches.

Dawn was not marked by the familiar burst of beauty and life; we were awakened by the furious patter of the rain's little fingers on the tent-cloth, and by that strong smell of decay which comes from forests when it rains. As usual, opinion was divided as to the best course to pursue—to give up right away, or to keep on hoping. In the end, hope won the day, and only two of the party refused to leave camp.

We had hardly started when the fog did its utmost to lift, and the sun, whether as a mark of goodwill or the height of duplicity, managed to filter through the cloudy ceiling. However, long skeins of mist still trailed below the hamlet; it would have been foolish to have any illusions about the worth of this clear-up or its duration. But we decided to profit by it as much as possible and go straight up the steep Coin Charnier valley.

This forced march was not particularly appreciated, and the most discontented of the whole party was, of all people, my old friend Marcel Ichac, who only yesterday had been amusing us with tales of the toil and trouble he had met with in the course of the interminable approach-march with the French Himalaya Expedition, of which he had been one of the members and instigators two years before.

The caravan climbed rapidly up towards the moraines of the Coin Charnier glacier, crushing the sodden grass, moss and rhododendrons beneath its feet. Scraps of cliff burst through their tunic of fog and appeared here and there as though hanging in the turbulent sky; mists crept stealthily along the depths of Valsenestre. None the less I relished the pungent flavour of this savage landscape, like one of those Alsatian wines which some palates cannot stand.

But the weather conditions called for another staff-conference, and in the mountains as in diplomacy coalitions are a weakening factor; opinions as usual differed.

" Seeing how far we've got," said some.

" We might as well get back before it turns really bad," retorted the others.

So the party broke up again; I was going on with three companions, and three more were turning back. As for Ichac, original as always, he would do neither one thing nor the other; he would wait for us on the spot, wrapped in his cloak, after fixing a place to bivouac and constructing an imposing and strangely-shaped cairn, just like the ones, so he assured us, the natives built in the Himalayas. I christened it the " Tibetan cairn " right away.

So my party, reduced to less than half, prepared to attack its objective, and started off along the left side of the Coin Charnier glacier. As this made a right-angle bend higher up, all we had to do to reach the upper portion was climb the crumbling wall which supported it, an easy ascent through the continual coming-and-going of the clouds. We soon got back to the glacier and made our way along the left bank above the cliff we had just climbed. Contrary to the opinion we had formed of it from below, the slope of the glacier was quite steep, and as far as we could make out through rifts in the fog it accentuated rapidly. After a climb of about five hundred feet, made without too much trouble over the rocks along the edge, we reached the point, close on ten thousand feet up, where the promontory comes up against the Pointe de Coin Charnier. From there on the ascent would be much more difficult, and we needed to be able to see clearly in order to select the best route.

We decided to have a snack on a comfortable terrace while awaiting the necessary break in the clouds, but in its place there came a sudden heavy storm of cold, wind and snow. Hail spattered against the rocks all around and stung our faces and hands like needles. In a few moments our determination to " see it through " had met its match; quite obviously the mountain wanted none of us

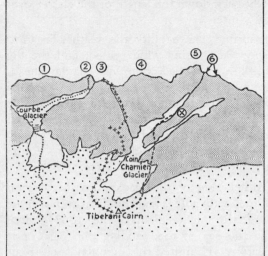

Diagram 5

POINTE SWAN GROUP

(10,807 feet)

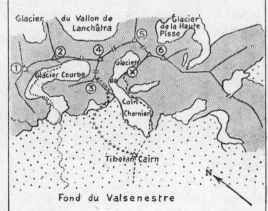

Fond du Valsenestre

Timetable

FIRST ATTEMPT ON
POINTE SWAN

Valsenestre	7 a.m.
Tibetan Cairn	9 - 10 a.m.
Limit of the Attempt ⊗	Noon - 1 p.m.
Valsenestre	4 p.m.

POINTE MARGUERITE

Valsenestre	5 a.m.
Foot of the Glacier	8 - 9 a.m.
Summit	11 a.m.- Noon
Valsenestre	3 p.m.

that day. We went swiftly back down the length of the glacier over rocks which were already white.

And then, with truly feminine changeability, the weather began to improve; the whirling snow and biting wind ceased, and the fog broke up to disclose both the way we had come and what lay ahead. In all fairness, we were bound to admit that the point we had reached was the end of the approach, and that the only difficulties of the course, which appeared to be quite considerable, were to be found in the last thousand feet. We should have had to climb diagonally across the upper wall as far as the Pointe de Coin Charnier—Pointe Swan gap, and beyond that cover a pretty jagged arête.

Opposite us, on the other side of the glacier, Pointe Buisson spread a frowning cliff, seamed with gullies and ribs, like an enormous pleated black veil. Ahead, the mighty prow of the group, Pointe Royer, ploughed through the sea of fog, sending the foam of it splashing back along its flanks. I admired this mountain's clear-cut profile, up which I had several times already traced a possible route from a distance.

We bounded down the cliff below the glacier, now streaming with water and melting snow. At the Tibetan cairn we picked up our Himalayan, fast asleep, and went striding over the stones and the yielding vegetation back to our base-camp in the valley. The welcome our friends gave us was not entirely free from irony as we admitted our failure, which was made more laughable than ever by the return of the fine weather; our mountain was now queening it serenely in the clear evening light.

Still, the expedition left me with no feeling of bitterness. Rather it planted the seed of a desire to come back and explore this massif, and finish what we had started today.

2. Pointe Royer (10,499 feet) by its west and south faces

October 23rd, 1938.

My friend Le Ray, passing through Grenoble in July 1938, had invited me to accompany him in the course of the next month to Pointe Royer, whose magnificent virgin west wall he, like myself, dreamed of conquering. Our homes lay far apart, and we had never mentioned this project to one another during any of our infrequent meetings, so the coincidence of our desires was surely due not to pure chance, but to a certain alpine telepathy by which the spirit of the cordée was made manifest. Unhappily the duties and joys of approaching fatherhood prevented me from accepting my friend's offer, and the summer went by without my hearing whether or not he had been able to pull it off.

During the month of September the mounting world-wide concern over events in Czecho-Slovakia turned our eyes from the mountains, but presently the tension lessened again. The sun reappeared in the sky and in our hearts; October brought splendid weather, and every Sunday saw us starting off for our beloved heights. The longing to scale Pointe Royer came to me anew, like a desire too long suppressed.

In company with the cool and reliable René Nicolet and Charles Laffont, the ebullient Gascon, I left Grenoble by car about 4.30 in the morning on October 23rd, 1938, and two hours later we alighted in Valsenestre, on the road to the marble quarry. It was still thick night, but that made little difference, since Laffont and I both knew the way as far as the Tibetan cairn, having been over it only two months before. Going along, I told my two companions all about the fascinating cliff, still virgin if Le Ray had been unsuccessful, and irresistibly attractive in any case. The weather seemed favourable, though very misty. The day broke little by little during our tramp; the tired old sun hardly had the strength to climb into the sky. In the valleys the rust of autumn was eating up the meadows.

We reached the cairn, which marked the end of the approach, and made a longish halt to inspect the chosen cliff. It looked very fine from there, a trapezium in shape, with the lower portion divided in two by a buttress. We decided to climb the right-hand face and reach the promontory at the point where it abutted on the cliff; above that we should have to do what we could with the upper part, which the perspective prevented us from seeing.

Off we went. Some screes and remains of snowfields, which in summer are very much the shape of a white horse, took us to the foot of the great polished slabs which form the base of the cliff. We made our way along towards the south in search of their weak point, and a scramble up several tiers brought the cordée to the bottom of the southern face where the barrier of slabs was lowest.

Nicolet, our leader, put on his espadrilles and started up; he climbed carefully, for several holds had already given way. He

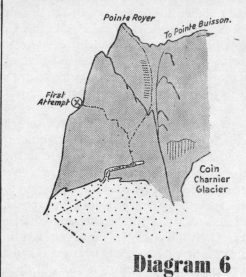

Timetable

Valsenestre	5 a.m.
Cairn	7.40-8.10 a.m.
Foot of Pointe Royer	9 a.m.
Limit of attempt	11.30 a.m. - Noon
Base of couloir	1 30 p.m.
Summit	2.40 - 3 p.m.
Valsenestre	6 p.m.

Diagram 6

POINTE ROYER
South-East Face

Diagram 7

POINTE SWAN
West Face

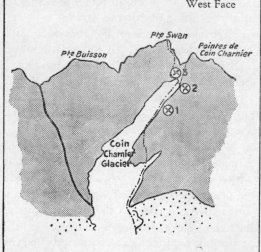

⊗ 1 ⎫
⊗ 2 ⎬ Limits of successive attempts
⊗ 3 ⎭

Timetable

(FOURTH ATTEMPT)

Valsenestre	4.15 a.m.
Cairn	8.20-8.40 a.m.
Summit	1.20 - 2 p.m.
Valsenestre	7.30 p.m.

settled himself firmly above, and one after the other we joined him, only to find that the next pitches were not at all what we expected; instead of the good solid rock we hoped for, there was an incredible jumble of steep slabs which looked as though they might collapse as soon as you looked at them. However, it was Hobson's choice; we had to make a slant across this frightful ruined wall to reach the top of the buttress which bounded it, nearly five hundred feet away to the left.

Never had our experience as old campaigners in the Oisans proved of more value; no holds gave way and there were no alarms, but it was a terrific strain on all of us. Moreover, the traverse required so much time and care that it was past noon when we reached the buttress—only to receive a crushing disappointment like a blow in the face. We were already pretty far up the cliff, but the remainder of it was something quite out of the ordinary; an almost perpendicular wall furrowed with narrow parallel cracks which made it look like a pipe-organ, overlooking a nasty sheer drop of over 700 feet. Above us, in the southern portion of the face, there was certainly a deeper and less airy fissure, but it was all slippery with ice. We decided unanimously, though not without rancour, that in view of the time and the nature of our previous difficulties there was nothing for it but to beat a shameful retreat.

I learned later that Le Ray had realised his project in August. He climbed the buttress itself to the point we had just reached, then continued his ascent by the fissures dominating it, which at that time were dry and provided some very interesting work.

The thin veils which had been floating in the air ever since day-break had now thickened and formed cloudy autumnal bands which came and went among the mountains. We started down, very depressed; a complete failure like this at the very end of the season would prey on our minds all winter. If the climbing of that face had been unpleasant enough, the descent was purely horrible; even with the aid of mere caricatures of rappels, we moved extremely slowly. Just before reaching the lower step of slabs, I noticed about 150 feet above us a gap in the arête which bounded the face to the south. Curiosity being one of the driving forces of my passion for mountaineering, I persuaded my companions to scramble up the two or three pitches necessary to gain this loophole and have a look at the other slope of Pointe Royer.

Imagine, then, my surprise at discovering, not a dozen yards beyond the gap, a magnificent couloir, quite dry and easy, which lost itself top and bottom in the fog. It was an irresistable temptation to which only our friend from Béarn proved insensible, so we struck a bargain with him; he would await us in the gap for a few minutes, (in actual fact he languished there nearly two hours) while we made a cursory inspection of this fascinating couloir.

In order to make all possible speed we decided to move together, since the easiness of the climb permitted it, and we rapidly gained height. The edges of the couloir were bordered with towering gendarmes. These queer pallid pilgrims came to meet us through the fog, leaned towards us, fell back and vanished, swallowed by the mists; each of us went our own way. At that pace three hundred feet were swiftly climbed. More cracks, slabs, easy pitches fled beneath our feet; the couloir still went on. The clouds seemed to be thinning; through the veil we could see, fifty yards higher, a phantom breach in a spectral arête. We realised that this was the one joining Pointe Royer to its neighbour, Pointe Buisson, so our goal must be just to the left of the couloir, within arm's reach.

This realisation multiplied our strength and our impatience tenfold; we scrambled feverishly up the fairly steep but easy wall which formed the right side of the couloir. Unfortunately I soon fell victim to this " French Fury "; a good-sized stone, dislodged by my companion's feet, hit me so hard on the thigh that I collapsed with the pain. I thought the bone was broken, and like a flash there went through my mind all the trouble and suffering that would come of it in a spot like this. Thank goodness, I got off with nothing worse than an enormous bruise, and by gritting my teeth I was able to go on after massaging it a bit.

The mist was thinning and evaporating about us as we climbed; you could see from its bluish tinge that there was fine weather just behind the faint screen. With the haste of a lover dashing to a rendezvous, the cordée, on edge with impatience, climbed a final pitch glazed with rime and ice, and came out on the summit into full sunlight under an exquisitely clear blue sky.

A few yards below us rolled a shifting sea of cloud, its long swell beating against the archipelago of peaks which emerged from it all around—Pointe Swan, Pointe Buisson, Pointe Marguerite, La Muzelle; as far as the eye could see there was nothing but waves and white horses. My beloved Oisans had not wanted us to part at loggerheads this year; after being plunged into the bitterness of failure, with delicate *coquetterie* we were given the victory we had despaired of, and so our pleasure in it was intensified.

The joy of the summit, the radiant satisfaction of a successful climb; there for us to whom the mountains are everything in life is Heaven's open door, like divine inspiration to an artist, ecstasy to a saint, or a great discovery to a scientist. When we come back to earth, we bring with us something that brightens our whole existence and provides endless happy dreams.

René and I knew such a fullness of delight on the peak that only the fog managed to drive us away, submerging our reef beneath a great comber. Our descent was rapid; drunk with joy we bounded from one side of the couloir to the other, sending down showers of stones. Our friend Laffont was perished with cold on his misty arête; he could hardly believe us as we told him in a few words of our great experience and how sorry we were he had not come with us. Then, since the light was failing, we completed the descent of the cliff at a brisk pace; the barrier of slabs gave us little trouble, and in the dusk we raced down the grassy slopes and hopped with more precaution through the screes of the Coin Charnier valley. We got back to the car as night fell.

Startled for an instant by the headlamps, the tall black firs of the Valsenestre forest seemed to flee into the night behind the car, steadily interposing themselves in greater and greater numbers between us and our climb, which was already fading into the marvellous world of dreams.

3. New Attempt on Pointe Swan

July 14th, 1939.

The interrupted attempt in 1938 seemed to linger round my kit like an odour of regret, and it hit me full in the face at the beginning of summer, 1939, when I got my ropes and axe out of their cupboard. There was nothing for it but to take the Valsenestre road again, and I arrived there by car at dawn on July 14th in company with my friend Jacques Chenais, who had knocked about all over the Oisans, and two others who had been with us in 1938.

As usual, the weather saw fit to turn foggy soon after dawn, throwing us all into a nerve-racking state of uncertainty. I know the clouds of my mountains so well; I have looked up at them times without number in a stubborn effort to wrest their secrets from them.

Lovely peaceful cumulus, long milky strands, black nimbus in sooty skies; clouds in wild disorder, great trailing scarves, rounded domes and immense flocks of white sheep—despite their promises, they have so often made a fool of me as a weather-prophet.

We were hardly at the Tibetan cairn before the Pic Turbat was swallowed up by dark wreaths and the Muzelle arêtes sliced off as though by a gigantic plane. My two friends did not feel in good form and gave up the idea of making the ascent, so I went on alone with Chenais; thanks to my knowledge of the region, I was able to climb rapidly as far as the point attained the previous year. Clouds and clear-ups followed one another, without either snow or rain.

Looking up, we traced an oblique route across the flanks of the Pointe de Coin Charnier, a little above the left side of the glacier, and attacked the cliff at once before the weather could get worse. The cordée gained height without much difficulty over some easy steps, then crossed the ruined arêtes dominating the glacier, whose steep incline could be seen through the yellowish fog. We detached some stones which went hurtling down like jackdaws on their prey, and we heard their muffled gallop hammering away at the icy slope.

Some couloirs filled with frozen snow cut across our path; we passed them by chipping out comfortable steps. More ruined arêtes, some polished slabs, several chimneys and a lot of uncertain holds; the cordée ought to be getting near the shoulder. Suddenly, in the mist, we came up against a gleaming slope, the head of the glacier without a doubt, pitched at an extreme angle and swept completely clean.

A break in the fog enabled us to see the far edge, over three hundred feet away, at the foot of the last rocky barrier below the gap; to cut steps all the way across in the hard ice would take more

THE PHOTOGRAPHS ON THE FOLLOWING PAGES

than an hour, so we tried to get around over the top. The reversed cordée tackled the rocks above. The mist was thickening again; it became almost sticky, with a sickly smell like rotten wood, and caused us a good deal of distress. We came to some cold smooth slabs; the rocks overlapped like the tiles on a roof and were getting harder and harder to climb. Chenais managed to get up a few yards further, but it was dangerous going.

Suddenly through the still air there fluttered some white flakes, which hesitated a moment, then began to fall gently, lightly, unflaggingly. We turned on our heel.

Carefully we retraced our steps down the way we had just come; the rocks were whitening at the will of the freakish wind. Lower down, the pace became swifter on easier ground; at the Tibetan cairn we got out of the clouds, which formed a heavy ceiling above our heads over the Valsenestre cirque. We strode rapidly down the valley and found our two friends in the village; the warm welcome of the proprietress of the modest but pleasant inn did something to dispel the bitterness of this second check.

After lunch, nursing my disappointment, I went out alone for a short stroll through the hamlet, which is almost abandoned. Where more than two hundred souls lived fifty years ago there are now less than a dozen. All the sadness of all the deserted countrysides of France is in those ruined homes where happy families once lived. Walls fallen, cellars littered, yards choked with vegetation, the village is slowly sinking back into oblivion, like gravestones eaten away by time and moss; tomorrow it will be nothing but a forsaken cemetery and soon even its name will be gone. The night wind will bring no sound from its silent, forgotten ruins but the whisper of the tormented soul of Valsenestre-the-Dead.

4. Pointe Marguerite (10.690 feet)

May 24th—25th, 1942.

This is a peak on the summit ridge, halfway between Pointe Swan and La Muzelle, also very little frequented.

The war had passed over us, spreading tragedy through our country and our family; we drank great draughts of the cup of sorrow. Then life began again, timidly, in a France torn apart and mourning.

Somehow I hesitated to revisit the mountains. I felt it would be sacrilege, like daring to pick flowers from a grave, to enjoy myself while there was still so much distress and suffering in the land and in the prisoner-of-war camps. But little by little a new conception dawned on me; the mountains might prove a balm to our wounds, a source of strength to our will, and a means of keeping our bodies fit to some more useful end. And so it came about that in the dreadful years after the war I owed my sole happiness in life to my family and to mountaineering.

I was impatient to see my beloved valleys of the Haut Valbonnais once again, not for themselves alone, but because they now had a new significance for us. While examining some family archives a short time before, my brother and I had in fact discovered to our surprise and delight that this region was the cradle of our family; one of our great-great-grandfathers, born at Le Désert in Valbonnais in 1775, had left his native village when very young to seek his fortune in the town. This unsuspected link filled us with pride, since in our eyes mountain blood was the finest possible, and justified both our special passion for climbing and my innate love for the western outskirts of the Oisans; unconsciously I had felt the mysterious call of the land of my forefathers.

So the feeling of making a solemn pilgrimage was added to the joy of revisiting this region.

In 1942 access to these valleys was comparatively easy in spite of the shortage of transport. My brother André and I cycled up to Haut-Valbonnais on the day before Whitsun; spring was already there in all its exuberance, chasing the last snows up towards the heights.

Pedalling along, head to wind, I let my thoughts stray back through my memories to the very beginning of what I may call my alpine life, to the time when I was brought from Paris to the mountains as a child, and the sight, from the depths of the valley, of the first snow-fields clinging to the flank of a wall and the green upland meadows running from the foot of the cliffs to the highest firs, made my heart pound with delight and longing as violently as an adult's does with desire. And every year it was the same ; silent, trembling with emotion, I felt the call of the mountains come to me. I firmly believe anyway that the motive power behind all passions springs from the same source; I remember a companion saying to me on one of our trips, as he looked at a glorious snow-slope sweeping up to the foot of a granite cliff :

"That excites me just as much as a naked woman."

But a truce to trifles; let us go back to our cycling approach. We arrived at Valsenestre as night was falling, intending to climb one of the peaks at the far end of the cirque next day. Unfortunately our attempt was thwarted by the rain which started before dawn, and we were glad enough to be able to find cover in the old ruined canteen of the marble quarry. Later it cleared up, and we spent the afternoon climbing the approaches to the Brêche de Valsenestre, which were new to us; stretched out there in the sun on some grassy platforms, we watched the evolutions of a herd of chamois.

Next day was a trifle more favourable, but the sky was still dangerously overcast at dawn, so we had to give up all idea of Pointe Swan, which we had thought of trying despite the heavy snow, and pick on something easier; Pointe Buisson, or one of the peaks overlooking the little Courbe glacier. We made our approach just above the remains of the old marble quarry, where the clear sound of the graving-tool has long since gone to join the murmer of the dying village in the past. The two of us ascended rapidly from ravines to promontories; at one point we had to shoulder and elbow our way furiously through an inextricable tangle of green alders laid flat by avalanches, which revenged themselves by puffing a strong smell of wet verdure in our faces.

We reached the moraines of the glacier before it was really light. Looking up from the last combes, we were struck by the peculiar shape of some of the rocks on an arête not far off, which were outlined against the pale dawn-washed sky. Our amazement increased as we saw them move and change shape again; we wondered for a moment whether like Peer Gynt we had strayed into the enchanted land of trolls. But the explanation was more prosaic; it was a herd of chamois standing quietly on the crest. They allowed us to come within a few yards of them, then unhurriedly, like graceful incarnations of those mountain nymphs, the Oreads, they bounded into a neighbouring combe and were lost to sight.

We tackled the base of the Courbe glacier; this region was new to me, so I was keeping a very interested eye on the configuration of the crests and their ramifications. During one brief pause on a rocky islet, I lost myself in conjectures upon the extraordinary living conditions of the glacier fleas, a number of which were skipping

51

about on a sheet of melting ice close by. Raising my eyes towards the sky, which was getting extremely murky, I pointed out to André the far-off eastern slope of the Clapier du Peyron, reminder of a happy climb together in Spring, 1938; and, opposite us, the stately south face of Pointe Royer, still filled for me with the unexpected joy we had plucked from it in the autumn of the same year.

But enough of reminiscences. We had to get on as fast as possible in order to reach one of the peaks on the summit ridge before the weather broke—and not miss the only train from Valbonnais which would land us back in Grenoble that night.

The Courbe glacier has a bottleneck and a small ice-fall between its upper and lower reaches, which entailed some interesting step-cutting under the glacial pediment and up a steep narrow couloir. A few dozen blows of the axe, and we were on the tranquil snowfields overlooking the séracs; above us the untidy crests tore the mist with their multiple spears.

We should have preferred to try Pointe Buisson, next to Pointe Swan and even more neglected by climbers, but the weather was threatening, so we had to confine our ambition to the nearest summit, Pointe Marguerite, whose south-west arête was quite close.

With turned-up collars and gloved hands, we scrambled upwards through the spattering hail. Slab and ruined arêtes, quite simple to negotiate, alternated with pitches of fresh snow in couloirs; this confused and broken ensemble was typical of the Oisans, and magnified our pleasure in this new contact with our beloved mountains. Near the summit, as if in compensation for our perseverance, the curtain of mist rent apart, and we looked down the sheer drops which mark the north slope of the massif to the vapours boiling up from below.

The hateful obligation of a strict timetable unfortunately compelled us to leave the icy peak long before we had had enough of it; permeated with the joy of the summit, we returned swiftly to the Courbe glacier and went striding down at speed. At the north foot of Pointe Royer we came across a queer little glacial lake, completely frozen at that time of year and quite unexpected at such a high altitude.

We glissaded down to the bottleneck and carried on again beyond it as far as the "chamois-crest." Ridiculous figures beneath the troubled sky, we descended unhurriedly, gossiping as we made our way down one slope after another. It was the first time since the war that we had been together in the Oisans, so it was natural that we should exchange notes on the short campaign we had both made in the Alps with the scouts while it was still fresh in our minds. The privileged conditions under which we had so served represented to us just one more favour from the mountains, since we had been spared the heartbreaking retreat across a France stricken with stupor.

Before we knew it we had reached the splendid shade of the Combe-Oursière forest, then Valsenestre. And so, after an interval of more than two years, our fraternal cordée, a threaded needle which has embroidered an arabesque of climbs all over the Oisans, found its way back to its beloved massif. Heaven send we may never forsake it again as long as we have strength to roam the mountains.

5. *Up Pointe Swan in the snow*

June 14th, 1942.

I have always had a horror of the unfinished; no matter how modest the goal, be it work, study, exploration, mountain-climb, I pledge myself unconsciously to see the thing through to the end. So the completion of the trip up the west slope of Pointe Swan, which I had already attempted twice, kept thrusting itself insidiously into my mind.

At the beginning of summer, 1942, my favourite climbing-companion, Le Ray, agreed to accompany me on a fresh try, not, however, without expressing his entire lack of enthusiasm for the project. During our cycle-trip up, a violent storm overtook us at Entraigues and obliged us to shelter for a whole hour, so that we did not finish our journey until after nightfall.

Before going to bed, I wanted to visit the hermits of the " Community of Valsenestre"; these two ardent proselytes, forsaking shortly after the armistice their cities of Lyons and Valence and their business of architect and contractor, had gone " back to the land " in the most forgotten village—it now comprised only three families—in the most deserted part of the country. They had faith in their enterprise, and being mountaineers themselves were as filled with love for the soil of this hamlet they were trying to rebuild as if they had been born there. Despite their keenness on work and the services they rendered, their few neighbours regarded them with suspicion, having little confidence that these townsfolk would become acclimatised in such an isolated valley, no matter how fertile the ground. Time alone will tell whether city-dwellers can turn peasant for good on the land they love, or whether the easier urban life will call them back once the war and the difficulties of food-supply are over.

It was still night when we left the pleasant inn; in the star-spangled sky we read the promise of a fine day ahead. Less than an hour later we were at the end of the Coin Charnier valley, but since daybreak we unfortunately no longer had any illusions about the weather; a very unpleasing fog trailed across Valsenestre, coming up from the south, and the dawn had been livid in a white-veiled sky. We should have to hurry again today to escape the storm and catch the evening train at Valbonnais.

The cordée's equipment was extremely heterogeneous; I had assured my companion that we were going to make a rock-climb, so we had brought only one axe, but Alain, despite my critical remarks, had absolutely insisted on burdening himself with a pair of crampons.

Under a leaden sky we doubled the Tibetan cairn, and tackled, a little above it, the névés which prolonged the Coin Charnier glacier, where the low temperature had kept the snow very hard. Triumphantly Alain donned his crampons and went up like a bird, whilst I, axeless and treading on the edge of my soles, gingerly walked the tight-rope. I could not possibly keep up with him on such terrain, so I told him not to wait for me.

" See you at the bottom of the upper Coin Charnier cliff, old man ! "

He was already a long way ahead, and easily followed the course of the little hanging glacier; I got off it as quickly as I could on to the rocks on the left bank, and scrambled swiftly up the crumbling wall I had already climbed twice before the war. I found Alain wrapped in his cloak near the point reached on my first attempt; in an icy wind he had been studying the problem of the climb while awaiting my arrival. Opposing my plan of attack via the rocky left flank of the Pointe de Coin Charnier, he suggested instead that we climb the glacier at its steepest point as far as its head, and scale the rock barrier above leading to the Pointe Swan—Pointe de Coin Charnier gap.

" But, Alain, we've only got one axe and one pair of crampons."

" I'll cut you some good steps, and you can have my hammer."

" O.K. Let's have a shot."

The slope was terrific, and it got worse. The snow, still very hard, was covered here with a thin coat of frozen pellets which must have fallen the day before during the storm we had sheltered from at Entraigues. As for the rocks on either side, they were not much better; above this height they were completely glazed, a fact which would not make things any easier for us. We had arrived too late at Valsenestre the previous night and started out too early this morning to become aware of the extremely unfavourable state of the mountain.

Despite the bad conditions, the ascent of the glacier was made safely enough; Alain's steps were ample for me, and my companion, covering each pitch very quickly, thanks to his crampons and axe, carved out a comfortable platform each time from which to belay my advance. While we struggled, flattened against the snow, to gain height with all possible speed, creeping wreaths spilled over the arêtes, stole down the slopes, drifted round the cordée, swallowed it and pursued their stealthy course; a milky luminosity penetrated with difficulty into this two-dimensional, unrelieved world. We went on climbing by guess in the cotton wool.

" Land-ho ! " shouted my friend, who had glimpsed a rocky islet at rope's length.

We worked towards it, but the anticipated shelf turned out to be nothing but a much-inclined promontory dripping with silver thaw. However, true terra firma was not far off, and another pitch brought us to the foot of the rocky barrier, transformed by yesterday's storm into a cataract of ice.

The beginnings of a ledge looked attractive; my companion tackled it, cutting steps as best he could for his ill-equipped and thoroughly unhappy second. Our benumbed hands groped through the superficial snow, and the ice it covered, in search of holds hidden beneath the gleaming layers; progress was incredibly slow in the face of the difficulties and the precautions necessary in such terrain. Face glued to the cliff, I belayed my friend's tedious advance, endeavouring in accordance with the classic rules to keep the rope around some rocky projection, but these were all so glazed with ice that they offered little help in the event of a fall. While the " string " moved along loop by loop, I stared at the rock through its transparent casing, and a silly thought flashed across my mind : " It must be suffering horribly ! "

But a shake of the rope interrupted my pointless reflections on mineral physiology. " Come on ! Your turn ! "

We intended to follow the ledge, which got narrower and narrower and more and more slippery and afforded only vague ice-covered bosses by way of handhold, to the point where a rib cut across our horizontal path, and then scale the flank of this. Now and again, a stone broke with a crack from its bed, bounced off into space and disappeared; we would see it three hundred feet below, ploughing down the slope of the glacier with a bone in its teeth. My extreme instability gave me the feeling that it might not be long before we followed in its tracks; in my mind's eye I could picture the successive rebounds of our bodies, and even the hammering they would get if this came about.

My companion advanced another rope's length, with a great rasping of crampons.

Despite the deceptive foreshortening caused by the angle, we estimated that we were still at least two hundred feet below the Pointe Swan—Pointe de Coin Charnier arête, and at the present rate of progress it would take nearly an hour to reach it; from there to the summit, probably as much again, and then the descent of these pitches would take about half the time spent in climbing them. As it was nearly one o'clock already, it was a simple matter to calculate that we should not get back to Valsenestre before seven p.m., with the cheerful prospect of having to cycle fifty miles.

So it was about-face again, and for the third time I knew the bitterness of starting a descent without having gained the summit. I had made scarcely fifty yards elevation on my 1939 attempt, and a hundred and fifty on the 1938 one; here was a mountain which certainly seemed to want none of me.

As if to help us make up our minds without unnecessary delay, the weather broke completely; snowflakes began to fall with such slowness, continuity and regularity, that they conjured up for me fleetingly the idea of perpetual motion. Our descent of the face produced a brief moment of excitement; a large stone, suddenly loosened from its foundations, started wobbling just above my friend and threatened to sweep him away. But in a flash he had flattened himself with might and main against the wall, out of its trajectory, and the block fell past with a sound like thunder.

At the end of the ledge, which was more slippery than ever, we got back on to the glacier; our tracks were already beginning to be covered, and the damnable fresh snow balled treacherously on our soles. You dared not let your attention stray for the fraction of a second. Lifeless hands buried deep in the superficial layer, body glued to the slope, I climbed down like an automaton; three violent kicks at the supposed position of the old step, tread on it, then three more kicks and another step . . . My mind was a complete blank; I was absolutely unconscious of anything beyond the descent. While Alain was coming down, following cautiously in my tracks on account of the snow balled between the points of his crampons, I took in the stiff frozen rope like a fisherman hauling in a net; my aching hands sent lumps of ice rattling off it.

Eventually we came back, miserably, to the bleak rocky bank at the point where we had left it that morning. There was at least one practical conclusion to be drawn from this new check; contrary to my belief, the difficulties of this trip were icy rather than rocky, a fact which Alain had foreseen, and his crampons had been essential to our safety.

There followed the sad and disillusioned climb down the crumbling wall, once more dripping with rain. Never again would I return to this cross-grained, harsh Pointe Swan, which repulsed me with as much regularity as an austere old maid—me, one of her very few admirers. The sight of the black precipices and jagged arêtes, glimpsed for a moment between two drifts of mist, which once had fascinated me by their savagery, today revolted me. No, decidedly it was all over and done with. This massif had discouraged me for good and all; I should never come back to it . . .

So much hard work for another check. And yet, why should I attach so much importance to a few feet of cliff which the storm and the flight of time had prevented me from climbing ? After all, I had spent a whole day in a wild and primitive spot which was very dear to me, just the two of us in delicious solitude, and the expedition had served to reinforce yet once again a staunch mountaineering friendship that was already twelve years old. This heartfelt union with your climbing companion is moreover surely one of the purest joys of the whole business. Later on, when the multitudinous details of these courses had lost themselves in the past, we should be able to recall them for one another, bringing out devoutly from their time-tarnished case the jewels of our finest hours in the mountains.

Comforted by these philosophical thoughts and diverted by my friend's conversation, I hardly noticed the descent; little by little the bitterness of this fresh defeat melted from my heart. Back in the hamlet, I turned instinctively towards the unkind peak, and like those young mothers who have sworn during their labour never to bear another child, none the less once the worst is over begin to talk about " My next baby . . .," I surprised myself by saying to my companion,

" Next time I come back . . ."

6. A Summit like the rest

September 6th, 1942.

So there was a " next time," and it was not long delayed; before the summer was out I was off again along the road I had already taken thrice without success.

" Why," some of you will think, " why such determination over an undistinguished climb on a secondary peak or less ? "

In fact, why so much obstinacy ? An old score to settle, in the first place; then the carrying-through of a task on which I had absolutely set my mind. I should have hated to abandon the exploration of this new route up Pointe Swan; an inconsiderable peak it might be, but its vast solitude and great mystery made it extremely attractive.

As the years go by, I feel growing up in me an irresistible misanthropy, which naturally pushes me towards the less frequented and therefore secondary mountain-systems. Moreover, the really great climbs and out-of-the-ordinary routes are practically closed to me; firstly, because they call for a standard to which I cannot pretend; and secondly, because they involve risks incompatible with my family duties. Yet these big expeditions have disturbed my dreams more than once; the sight of those superb cliffs, all the more desirable since they are utterly beyond my reach, has so often made me wish that I could leave my body and let my spirit ramble in that perpendicular world to the end of time, tasting the savour of the forbidden fruit.

Thoughts straying, I tramped up the Coin Charnier glacier on a misty September morning, accompanied this time by my friend

Georges Franck. The dawn ascent of these deserted valleys reminded us both of the time, eight years before, when we had climbed La Muzelle together, by this same slope and in this same season. During those years so much had happened to us and our country; only the mountains and our love for them had remained unchanged.

We reached the glacier's upper basin very quickly; I knew every stone on the path by now. What a transformation since my last visit! It hardly looked like the same mountain. The slope was completely bare and split by several series of yawning *rimayes*; our ice equipment was going to come in very handy. We put on our crampons and Franck, who was a real crack, climbed swiftly and safely upwards; at first we both moved together, but one at a time became the order of the day as the gradient increased.

The second *rimaye*, gaping the whole width of the glacier, forced my companion into some hard step-cutting along the left side, under the Pointe de Coin Charnier face; while he was going slowly up, I belayed him as well as I could and kept a watchful eye on the slope from which stone-falls might be expected.

Then suddenly, brushing the arête which loomed above us, disturbingly low clouds began to march across the sky in rapid array, flinging themselves on Pointe Swan, rebounding, filling the combe, and submerging us in their whirling billows. Once again our world became nothing but a globe of mist, where everything seemed vague and shifting and warped in the semi-darkness; once again the mountain was giving me a sinister welcome. But it made no difference; today I was determined to see it through.

The fog was so thick that it was impossible even to see the steepness of the slope. Hacking away, Georges brought us to the rocky barrier, and there was the ledge where Alain and I had battled so hard three months before. The change here was all in our favour; despite the angle of the face the climb would be easy over the bone-dry rocks. Crampons, rucksacks and axes were left on a platform; on the off-chance I put my espadrilles in my pocket and led off with a rush, anxious to reach the summit before the threatened bad weather laid firm hold on the mountain.

In a few minutes we had traversed the whole length of the ledge which had called for the strictest care in June, but instead of climbing up the flank of the rib which intersected it, I decided to cross it, and there to my great delight discovered an easy, pebbly, couloir just beyond. We were going so well that we put it behind us in no time, and were soon nearing the crest. Above that there remained only a short climb, face or arête, I did not know which, and I should stand atop Pointe Swan at last.

A few final struggles; we could now see the Haut Valjouffrey through fugitive rifts in the boiling sea of cloud. The slope stiffened, but the rock was still excellent and climbing easy. Some chimneys, some faces, and then quite simply we came to the long-desired peak, marked by a tumbled cairn and the remnants of the pole left there fifty years before by Lord Swan, first visitor to this summit. And that was the end, the net result of so much effort—a few frosty stones lost in the mist. Maybe, but now my mind was at rest and I could turn contentedly to the many other peaks which still called me.

In one way this victory was different from all others; it brought peace to my heart rather than keen joy.

While my companion, anxious to carry away a tangible souvenir, was trying to take advantage of the breaks in the clouds to snap some pictures, I was curious enough to explore a few yards along the arêtes, the still-virgin north-west, and the south-east, which is the normal means of access to the summit. Then, following the tradition, we allowed the beast in us, which had suffered sorely since five o'clock that morning, to have his rights—complete relaxation of tired muscles and a relative satisfaction of hunger and thirst.

Tearing the clouds to the southward appeared the Pointe de Coin Charnier; it evoked for Georges and me a common memory, already drowned in the stream of the past. In company with Alain Le Ray and my brother we had left Le Désert in Valjouffrey, at Whitsun 1935, to climb Pointe Swan—even so far back !—by its southern arête. After a long slog through the snow, which was very heavy at that time of year, and a struggle with ice-glazed rocks, the caravan had painfully attained the Pointe de Coin Charnier and given up all idea of pushing on to its goal, which was protected by terrible corniches . . . The cherished alpine past spreads precise facts, solid memories across our flurried lives, like breakwaters against which the invading and destructive tide of forgetfulness beats in vain.

Before the imperious demands of time forced us to leave the peak, we cast a last glance around the horizon; with subtle *coquetterie*, the Haut-Jouffrey tore aside its veils of mist and displayed the triumphal route which leads by way of Fond Turbat to the Temple of the God of the Oisans, the immense and savage Pic d'Olan.

The descent went briskly, and we were soon back on the big ledge. As I worked along it, I could not help regretting that the shortage of time, and the excess of fresh snow three months ago, should have compelled us to turn on our heel at the very moment when the difficulties due to the most unfavourable condition of the mountain had been practically overcome.

The bad weather which had been hanging about since the morning now seemed ready to break loose; the cordée was engulfed once more by the yellow fog which seems to haunt these regions and be very much at home there. Crampons on our feet, we returned along the way we had come that morning, revelling in Georges' comfortable steps; it started to rain, and an icy dampness pierced us to the marrow. Presently a breeze swept the glacier, blowing away the fog and disclosing the sheer cliff of the Pointe de Coin Charnier looming over us.

One after another we plunged downward, glueing ourselves to the slope while our companion belayed. I was first across the *rimaye*; while Georges was coming down I secured his retreat from below, at the same time keeping an anxious eye on the rocks which prolonged the ice slope higher up. Their overlapping strata gave them the appearance of actually overhanging, and their black layers, all aglisten with water, looked full of menace; the rain could hardly fail to cause some stonefalls, and I was gripped by foreboding.

Suddenly, like horrible black birds, a flight of boulders plunged down the cliff, rebounded from the glacier and passed with a roar between Georges and me—instinctively flattened against the slope. Just like a woman who has finally surrendered, the mountain, conquered at last by sheer dogged persistence, was throwing us the inevitable, " I don't know what you must think of me ! " After that we had several more alarms, but the missiles were further off; the aim was certainly pretty wild. I admit I was scared of this slope; we were too much like condemned men, setting ourselves up as Aunt Sallies and taking our chance. But the feeling vanished as we reached the rocks, where we took off the rope and raced down at great speed.

And so at last I had made the climb on which I had set my heart, and from which three failures had not turned me. " It's proof

positive that mountaineering develops will power and tenacity,"
some of you may think. Not at all. Let nobody speak to me of
the educative virtues of climbing. I do not believe in them myself,
and in fact I even deny them; you come to the mountains *with*
your moral qualities, and *because* you have them, not to acquire
them. After almost twenty years of climbing and mixing with
fellow-enthusiasts, I do not know of a single idealist among us who
goes in for difficult and dangerous climbs with the idea of improving
himself.

Every nation moreover finds in mountaineering an expression of
its underlying taste; to those perpetual playboys, the French, it is
no more than a fine healthy distraction; to the English, the practice
of an exciting sport, and to the Italians a manifestation of roman-
ticism. It is, on the contrary, a much more serious matter to the
Germans; mountaineering to them, besides being a source of
national prestige, is a means of toughening-up, of preparing body
and soul for war. It is a fact that in their tales of climbing they
seem set on giving their readers, to use the colourful words of my
British friend, Maxwell Fleming, "The impression that they've
got hair on their chests." For them alone, perhaps, the mountains
are a means rather than an end.

If the climber does gain some qualities in the practice of his
art, so much the better, but they are only incidental and not the
reason why he does it. On the other hand, much petty meanness
sometimes spoils the alpine spirit; jealousy, back-biting and dis-
paragement, born of poor performance, are unfortunately only
too common.

The small-time climber really draws the sympathy much more
than those who go in for it in a big way; he may not have a monopoly
of itineraries on a heroic scale, but at least his love of the mountains
is purer since it is free from all competitive spirit.

" But look here, old chap," you may say, " wasn't it a brand-new
climb you claim to have made up Pointe Swan, and aren't all the
others you describe in this book ' firsts ' of some sort ? Well then,
as far as you're concerned, there's no more to be said."

Epilogue. In February 1943, with my inseparable companion
Alain I climbed the Taillefer, not far from Grenoble, on skis, as
training for our projected winter ascent of Pic Gaspard. At the
summit we met two skiers from La Mure, and an alpine fellowship

sprang up between the two parties in the white solitude. We happened to speak of the high valleys of the Oisans close to La Mure, and my love for Valsenestre found an echo in them; the name of Pointe Swan came up.

" Well, what a coincidence ! " said one of them.   " I climbed that too by the Coin Charnier glacier, last July."

Two months before us !

So after all he had stolen by a few days the thunder which had been thrice denied me, and which nevertheless had been waiting for centuries.   Thus may you get a lesson in modesty from a heap of stones !

Chapter Four

"TERRA INCOGNITA"

Pointe 3220 (10,565 feet). October 5th, 1942. *This peak is on the chain running from Lauranoure to the Pic Signalé, which separates the Lanchâtra valley from the Mariande. The recent survey map calls it " Pointe des Liches," and the neighbouring summit to the north " Pointe du Salude." In reality, according to the local inhabitants and the Coolidge guide, this latter name should apply to the summit called by the cartographer " Pointe Sud de Lauranoure," and the former to that designated " Pointe du Salude "; it seems that the names of these mountains have all been shifted one place south in order to christen an anonymous peak.*

Do you ever remember poring over one of those maps yellowed by the centuries, full of regions then unexplored ? The mapmaker, for want of anything better, has written " terra incognita " and

THE PHOTOGRAPHS ON THE FOLLOWING PAGES

25. From left to right: the eastern peaks of the Soreiller, the Pointe d'Amont, and the central and western peaks. In the background: l'Etret, Les Fétoules, L'Aiguille d'Olan, Pointe Maximin, and Les Arias. Seen from Pointe Thorand
26. From left to right: the Pointe d'Amont, the central and western peaks of the Soreiller, the Plat de la Selle: from the Selle refuge
27. The last slabs beneath the summit
28. A ledge on the cliff
29. Pic de la Fare, Romanche slope. The central peak is the culminating point of the massif
30. The east face of the Moucherotte from the Forges Valley
31. The peak
32. Friend of good and bad days

drawn a few mountains haphazard across them. Dreaming over these parchments, I can never help but envy the men of those far-off times, and regret that I was born too late in a world where the unknown has been pushed further and further away. Today our old earth has practically no more secrets to conceal from the avidity of her inhabitants; little by little they have reft them from her. Yet, deep in the heart of me, the desire for adventure, inborn heritage from my distant ancestors, forever burns with a flame as steady and enduring as an altar-lamp.

Mountain exploration, especially in the Oisans, our least known massif, offered something to satisfy this lust for the unknown, even though on a reduced scale. The foolhardy routes up the immense flanks of the kings of the massif are unhappily forbidden me, so I turned less daringly to the secondary peaks which adorn the " nooks where nobody goes." The discovery of new climbs in these modest " terræ incognitæ " often gave me intense joy, and (God forgive me!) a certain explorer's pride. After all, not everybody can afford a trip to Tibet or the Antarctic.

One day this thirst for novelty in mountaineering put me on the track of something important. The Oisans still held a summit worthy of the name which might be virgin; if so, it was certainly the last and there was no time to be lost. This pearl of great price, said to be around 10,565 feet in height, was quite close to Saint Christophe, just behind Lauranoure. In 1935, during the course of a climb up the Pic du Salude, and in 1937 and 1938, while scaling the latter's eastern spur, I had noticed this well-marked peak, which was separated from us only by the notch of a gap, and a photograph taken from the opposite side showed it firmly seated on its foundations.

At the time, having consulted the Coolidge guide and found that it was simply marked " No information," I had vaguely suspected that it must still be virgin. Later, in September 1942, while reading the proofs of the wonderfully complete guide to the Oisans complied by my friend L. Devies, I was struck by the fact that there was a blank for this peak instead of a description of the itinerary. At that moment my suspicion became conviction and I determined to try the ascent, even though the climbing season was almost over.

My brother André expressed the desire to take part in the adventure, so I put off the project until the beginning of October; we should then be reunited by a pious pilgrimage to a grave newly closed on the best of us, my father, servant of his country to the end of his strength.

So, on October 4th we arrived at Saint Christophe, André and I, at the end of the afternoon, after an exhausting bicycle ride. The night was going to be a short one so far as we were concerned. Before we turned in, a talk with our friend the guide Devouassoud Gaspard strengthened our hope that the desired summit was untrodden, but we were warned that we should have to contend with fresh snow, which had recently fallen as far down as the village, but had luckily been driven back to the heights by the sunshine of the previous days.

Quarter to four. Still half-asleep we left the hamlet, all dead and drowned in the night. Thousands of silver nails twinkled tirelessly in the clear frosty sky. Minds blank, eyes burning with sleep, we went down towards the Vénéon. My dulled brain cursed yet once more at the damnable five-hundred-foot descent, meditating on the advantage it would be, in more senses than one, to be able to avoid the bed of the torrent by a long footbridge or an aerial tramway.

Hobnails grated and axes clinked against the smooth round pebbles of the path, whose chaos seemed even worse by night than by day. We made our way steadily down to the Vénéon, which whispered its eternal confidences in the gloom; there at last was the culvert, and the ascent began.

The team climbed step by step. It was so dark that we had to let our feet guide us, striving not to lose the track. With slow movements of the shoulders we clove the thick tide of the night; the weight of the stars was light on our heads.

Through the shadows we glimpsed the livid face of the Alpe du Pin chalet, eyes wide-open and dead; the shepherds had abandoned it to its pre-winter solitude several weeks before. Above it, in order to reach the Ser de la Cochette, a fine bench which leads from the Alpe to the Mariande, we had to struggle in deep darkness against an ill-timed rocky barrier. And not far from the chalet the path maliciously saw fit to glide surreptitiously along the foot of a steep rise while we were looking for it above.

The tramp continued. The enormous silence weighed on our spirits. A thin sliver of moon emerged from behind the Ecrins; heavy clouds trailed across her face like slow-drifting ice-floes, and under her milky light we moved in an unreal world full of long

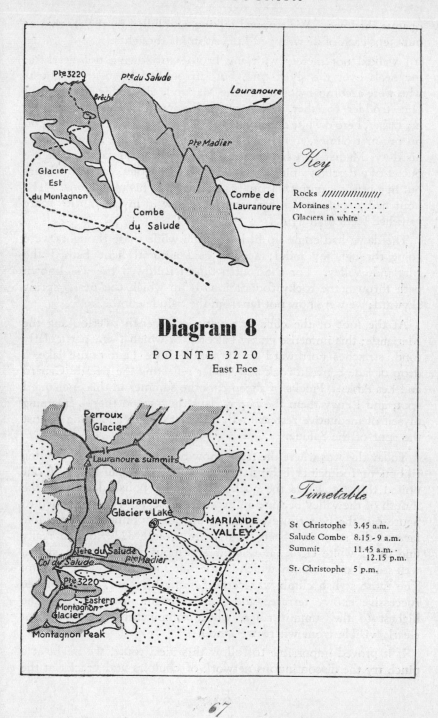

Diagram 8

POINTE 3220
East Face

Key

Rocks //////////////////
Moraines ·.·.·.·.·.·.·.·.
Glaciers in white

Timetable

St Christophe	3.45 a.m.
Salude Combe	8.15 - 9 a.m.
Summit	11.45 a.m.
	12.15 p.m.
St. Christophe	5 p.m.

opaque shadows. We stopped talking, and lulled by the rhythm of our steps each of us wrapped himself in his thoughts.

I walked not merely with my brother, following noiselessly at my heels over the short turf, but surrounded by beloved ghosts who were accompanying me to the Mariande along this path we had once trodden together. They were all very near and dear to me ; my father, hero despite defeat and captivity, Pierre Moch, companion on my first climbs, mown down in June 1940 while bravely doing his duty, Madier de Champvermeil, who fell during a climb at the outset of a dazzling alpine career, and René Nicolet, eating his heart out in a prison-camp, far from his country and his mountains. The hour had already struck for me when I saw in my memories more vanished faces than living.

The dawn had come up little by little while these thoughts were going through my mind; a clear cold autumn light bathed the Mariande valley. For the fourth time I followed the well-known path through the rocky foundations from which the peaks spring skyward; we were now not far from the Salude combe.

At the foot of the cliffs is a very long bench overlooking the Mariande; this immense grassy balcony, of which I am particularly fond, stretches northward as far as the little Lauranoure lake, a drop of jade between rock and glacier reflecting the Bec du Canard and Les Arias. Flocks of sheep pass the summer in this enchanted spot, and I envy them the happy days they spend there, dreaming myself of meditative retreat in an imaginary cabin snuggling against the spur of the Salude.

Today this was where the fresh snow began, and we left a winding ribbon of footprints behind us, a sort of materialisation of our united thrust towards the goal. A heap of polished slabs at the mouth of the valley became an excellent observatory from which to figure out the best route to follow up our mountain's inscrutable face to the summit. Seen from there, Pointe 3220 looked really fine in its white cloak; it was an enormous trapezium in shape, well-seated on a plinth which stuck out like the bow of a ship. The most stylish climb was certainly up this spur, scaling three successive snowy terraces and going straight upwards from the highest to the summit ridge, whose culminating point was not clearly visible from where we stood.

If it proved impossible to follow this ideal route, we might at a pinch try the discontinuous network of couloirs and cracks at the bottom of the east Montagnon glacier; as a last resort this would undoubtedly take us to the summit ridge, but a long way from the peak. So the best thing was to have a determined shot at the first of these two routes. The sun had melted the snow from the steepest rocks, and it might perhaps not be too much of a nuisance. It was already nine o'clock, and high time we were off; our three-quarters of an hour halt was out of all reason.

Slogging through the snow, the caravan started up the Montagnon glacier and skirted several treacherous half-filled crevasses. We could scarcely take our eyes off the unknown cliff, so impatient were we to attack it and avid for its secret. Should we be able to blaze a trail up this face despite the serious difficulties it seemed to present ? In any case, the rock which formed it was most attractive both in appearance and colour.

To reach the first terrace of the spur we had to climb a wall of slabs which were not unduly steep but perfectly polished and slippery. Over ground like that you have to smell your way laboriously, climbing here, traversing there, coming down several yards to try your luck elsewhere. However, the cordée gained the bench in a very few minutes and crossed it, plunging knee-deep in the fresh snow.

A second rock slope followed, steeper, and furrowed from top to bottom by an inclined chimney, not far from the junction of the spur with the cliff proper. It was pretty discouraging to look up from there at the wall which lifted skyward above the second terrace; it was all vertical slabs of fine brown rock, cracks, and overhanging chimneys; a long candle of ice dripped from a fault. " If we've got to climb that ! " Jackdaws were gliding and diving all along this cliff; lucky beings to have such an easy life and such a place to live!

I climbed the chimney which gave access to the second terrace with an impatience closely allied to anxiety. Its upper portion was a really sporting passage, where an overhang insistently posed the problem of balance. I could hardly wait to get out and make a few steps across the vast snowclad bench to see what lay beyond.

Heaven be praised ! There was no need to tackle the terrible precipice looming over me; an easy traverse would allow us to reach the final terrace and turn the flank of the ticklish wall. Ploughing calf-deep through the melting snow, we gained the third névé after getting the better of a narrow rock gully which had looked exceedingly difficult from further off. We stopped a few minutes to catch our breath and inspect the next pitches.

We were now at the foot of the last cliff, which was extremely steep and well over 600 feet in height; it soared straight up to the summit ridge with its array of pinnacles and gaps. To the right it reached as far as the Col de Salude; to the left, on the contrary, it was bounded by a faintly-marked arête quite close at hand. Climbing the cliff itself would be incompatible with the actual conditions, the little time at our disposal, and perhaps even our skill, but the arête which bordered it like a hem offered a distinct possibility of attaining the summit. In a few minutes we should be able to determine our chances of victory and being the first to set foot on this virgin peak.

Before starting the attack, we threw a glance at the spur coming from the Pointe de Salude, which developed from ours to the north and ran parallel to it; a shut-in valley like a deep furrow lay between the two. The promontory opposite seemed to have been split in twain by a mighty sword-stroke; in its lower part was a slender spire with abrupt sides—terra incognita—where Madier and Four-astier, new-haloed with their magnificent success on the north face of the Râteau, had accompanied Nicolet and me in 1938. Those days before the catastrophe already seemed very distant.

I shook off the cloak of memories; action in plenty awaited us.

A few paces towards the top of the névé, whose slope steadily increased, and we were at the foot of the arête we meant to scale. Owing to its exposure, the rock was covered with a snow-powdered casing of ice; half-a-dozen strokes of the axe sent flakes of ice flying and disclosed the holds buried under their cold cuirass. It was a typical " north face." We blew on our numbed fingers in the shade.

Several steps further, and I came out on the sun-drenched arête; we had only one thought: " What now ? " What I saw filled me with great delight, unheroic as it might be; against all expectation we were assured for the moment of an easy advance along the crest itself and the face which followed. This eastward cliff was quite clear of snow; it dominated the frightful wall we had been so much afraid of having to tackle when we started up the spur an hour before. We decided to take advantage of the easiness of the terrain and make up for lost time by moving together.

Through the loophole of a breach in the arête we cast an eye at the north-east face we had left not long ago; it was an almost vertical cliff, its centre bristling with strange elegant pinnacles hooded in snow; shadow was eternally queen there.

A few score more yards cheaply won, and our dash came to an end at the foot of a tall red-brown buttress whose weak point remained to be found. A rising traverse to the left brought me to an ice-quilted terrace. The best route from there was not so easy to decide; was it better to scale the thirty-foot slab, very nearly vertical and with the minimum of holds, or the frost-glazed crest gleaming not far away ? My preference pushed me rather towards the slab, which was at least dry.

It was an interesting, aerial and tricky climb. Towards the top it was necessary to make a traverse to reach a spacious platform, but try as I would, I could not manage to pull it off. I dare not, in fact, make a grab with a fingertip at a distant knob, when as a preliminary, I should have to let go the only hold worthy of the name anywhere in the vicinity. If only I had put on my espadrilles instead of leaving them in the bottom of my rucksack ! Three times I had a go at it just as you bring a balky horse back to the fence it has refused; this " tricky bit " was the sort of thing I particularly dislike because of the risks it entails. André finally came to the conclusion that he had better rescue me and save me a laborious descent; he climbed up the ice-glazed crest I had wrongly disdained, and got me out of my tight corner from above.

Another pitch without difficulty brought us to a wide cornice at the foot of a sheer wall of pure rock; I examined it closely in search of the best route, and made haste to change my boots for espadrilles in order not to repeat my previous error. At the same time, deep in my heart I addressed a passionate appeal to my father, whose memory had been with me the livelong day, that this obstacle might not halt us so close to our goal.

Meanwhile André had followed the shelf along, and was at rope's length when he discovered the vulnerable point; the cliff was split by a deep boxed-in chimney, with a high snowbank to help the climb. And having conquered this last wall without much trouble, we realised joyfully that nothing could now prevent us from attaining the summit ridge, whose rocks were silhouetted against the pale blue sky a hundred feet above. The vision gave me wings and in a few minutes I reached the crest of our mountain, my heart pounding with excitement.

But before stepping on to it, diving into the azure and looking at the nearby summit, I forced myself to wait several seconds, eyes closed, hardly able to contain my boundless impatience. It was the same as having a cup of fresh water in your hand after suffering a mighty thirst for hours, and prolonging your desire an exquisite instant more before wetting your parched lips.

Then my eager eyes opened on a steep arête, almost horizontal, which seemed to culminate in two towers separated by an angular gap. A slight disappointment at not having come out directly on the peak welled up in me, accompanied by a gnawing doubt, for on the further needle I had spotted a suspicious raised rock.

"Can that be a cairn?"

We approached our goal along the stone lace of the arête to a fine clatter of lumps rattling off on one side or the other. A few vigorous movements gave the cordée access to the first summit, a huge molar planted in the gum of the ridge; down we plunged into the notch, and we were at the peak itself, which seemed to welcome us with open arms. We let out a long yell of triumph.

André was close beside me, and his eyes betrayed his happiness. Laughing, I showed him the rock which from a distance I had taken uneasily for a signal. No, there was no smallest trace here of human hands; no mountaineer had ever touched the stones which we were piling as we sang. During all the twenty years we had been climbing, this was the first time we had reached a virgin summit; it gave us an intense feeling of pride and exaltation and also of communion, as though we had been admitted to the holy of holies, as though our favourite mountains had confided to us one of their last secrets.

The minutes flew by like wildfire as we sat there side by side, reverently savouring the healing peace of the summit. At our feet stretched the valley of the Mariande, caressed by the velvety autumn light; beyond, plastered with snow, their arêtes picked out with touches of sunshine, were the Bec du Canard, Les Arias, l'Olan, Les Fétoules . . . We had visited all these mountains of the Oisans and considered them rather as our backyard; each one seemed to say to us from afar off : "Do you remember?"

By winding a skein of memories about all these peaks we had saved a little of our youth from being swallowed in the gulf of time.

There is little to tell about our return over the now-familiar path. We retraced serenely, minds at ease, the passages we had approached with such anxiety not long before. Filled with joy both in body and soul, we came down to earth so lightly that the valley seemed to be lifting itself up to meet us.

Before leaving the Salude combe to plunge into the Mariande valley, we cast a long last look at the peak whose ascent would always remain one of our most cherished memories.   Today we had written a page in the logbook of our mountain escapades that was a very happy, if not very glorious one.   Whenever I can spare a moment from the worries and preoccupations of everyday life to leaf through it, it is very often the remembrance of this sunlit trip which comes to mind, just as a book opens by itself at the page most often read.

So now the tale of our Oisans was complete; by our visit to this peak we had wiped the words " Terra Incognita " from the yellowed map.   The humble mystery of the high places, fruit of my imagination, had really proved to be nothing more than those things we already knew so well, slabs and buttresses such as we had tackled hundreds of times.   Still, to have blazed a new trail, lifted the veil and appeased a burning curiosity, was a great reward for our efforts; my sheaf of mountain memories was enriched.

Let me admit that the memory of my father was closely linked with the whole trip; anyone who has been prematurely robbed of a beloved and admired parent by an unjust fate will understand me. It was the anniversary of the day, so near and yet already so far, when he left us, broken by defeat; he especially loved the Mariande, and his presence and his protection were very real to us all through our happy exploration.

It has therefore seemed to me natural, quite apart from any question of vainglory, to ask the competent topographical commission to give his name to the peak we scaled for the first time, which the mapmakers have mistakenly christened with the name originally given to a neighbouring summit.   It will be a balm for our sorrow and our filial piety if his memory as a mountain officer who died for France is thus perpetuated by a peak in the Oisans bearing forever the name, " Pointe Paul Boell."

Chapter Five

UP PIC GASPARD IN WINTER

March 5th and 6th, 1943. Pic Gaspard (12,743 feet) is the forward bastion, to the east, of the Meije group. The ascent in summer is of only moderate difficulty, but in winter the absence of any refuge at a sufficient height sets a real problem for would-be climbers.

We decided to pitch camp on a wide snowy shelf at the mouth of the Claire valley.

In radiant sunshine, cheek by jowl with the Dantesque precipice of La Roche Méane, we made leisurely preparations to bivouac, methodically trampling down the snow and laboriously scratching up clumps of dry grass, destined to insulate us from the cold ground. Our friend Jamet's Himalaya tent was unfolded, put in place and set up. While Alain, my rope-brother, went off to fetch water from a quarter-of-an-hour away, I finished the job, thinking over the circumstances of our trip as I worked.

We intended to try and make the first winter ascent of Pic Gaspard. It was a project that had been ripening for ten years without seeing the light of day; unfavourable conditions in the mountains, uncertain weather, and the impossibility of getting leave at the same time had made us put off the trip from season to season. Yet everything had been so much easier in those days.

Then came the black hours of the war; everything became difficult, complicated, almost impossible.

74

But somehow we had felt that the time was just right for the enterprise, not only for the climb itself, however fine it might be, but to prove to ourselves that we were neither demoralised by the obstacles which conditions put in our way, nor downcast by defeat. We wanted, moreover, to establish that our bodies, despite all privations and my companion's recent captivity, could still make an exceptional effort, and that we were still capable of making plans and carrying them through. In a word, we needed some big adventure to help us regain hope and confidence.

Impatiently we waited with expectant hearts till a series of fine days had made the heights practicable, and at last the departure date was fixed. Having got together the necessary stuff, equipment and food, not without trouble, we arrived at La Grave on March 4th. Out of prudence we had sought a third companion, but in vain; none of our friends in Grenoble was free or inclined to undertake the trip, so Alain and I were going to try it alone. Once more we should form a cordée which had so often known, in the Oisans, the bitterness of defeat and the intense joy of the summit.

At first our luck seemed to be out. The weather had been set fair for three weeks, but as soon as we got to La Grave an icy east wind, the Lombarde, began to blow furiously, and we had to put off our departure for a day. But on the 5th we were highly delighted to find when we woke that both wind and clouds had disappeared, and we left soon after eight o'clock, accompanied by a young porter to help carry our huge rucksacks up as far as the Cavales valley. We put on our skis a little beyond Villar d'Arêne, and wrapped silently in hopeful thoughts crossed the monotonous plains of the Pied de Col and the Plan de l'Alpe. Some threatening clouds were certainly coming up from the east as they had done the day before, but my friend displayed such sincere optimism that it would have been unkind to pull a long face. Besides, the topmost pyramid of Pic Gaspard, glimpsed for an instant at the mouth of the Vallon de l'Homme, had looked to be in perfect condition.

To give myself a little more confidence, I tried to persuade myself that this particular region had always been very lucky for me, by enumerating with a certain amount of complaisance my various successes in this massif. Anything goes when you start getting pessimistic!

Where the Platte aux Agneaux and the Cavales valleys cross is Valfourche, court of the temple from which the Romanche springs.

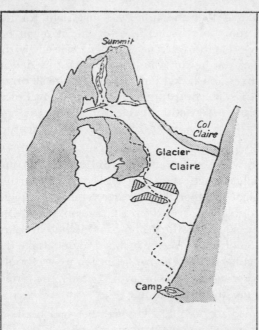

Key

Rocks ///////////////
Moraines ·:·:·:·:·
Glaciers in white

Timetable

	March 5th	
La Grave	8.30 a.m.	
Camp	3 p.m.	
	March 6th	
Camp	7.15 a.m.	
Rimaye	10.25 a.m.	
Summit	11.45 a.m.	12.15 p.m.
Camp	2.30 p.m.	4 p.m.
Villar d'Arène	7 p.m.	

Diagram 9

PIC GASPARD
(12,743 feet)
East Face

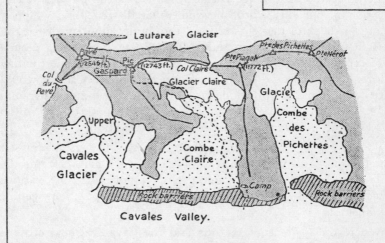

It was sheer delight to see once again the beloved Oisans cliffs, whose very shapes could evoke for us so many precious memories, moments of happiness or anguish, friendly faces quick or dead, all the lovely adventures of yesteryear. These mountains had become the book of our most splendid hours, each summit a page of that past which stayed whole despite the ravages of time. It was sweet to run our gaze over it and recapture the subtle perfume of the things which have been.

We clambered up the Combe des Cavales, and it became apparent at once that the lack of snow practically ruled out any danger of avalanches, and that our ascent of the passably dry southern precipices would be greatly facilitated. Lastly, the promise of fine weather was writ large in the radiant sky; tomorrow we might perhaps have the sort of trip you dream about.

At the foot of the rocky barrier of the Claire valley we thrust skis and sticks into a well-sheltered nook, and began to climb the thousand-foot slope which to my mind constituted the first difficulty of the trip. Luckily there was little snow and scarcely any ice, and I was able to find quite easily the route I had followed eleven years before. At the bottom of the " Mauvais Pas " we sent back our porter and added his load to our already heavy rucksacks.

In a few minutes we came in sight of the Claire valley, at three o'clock, somewhat ahead of schedule. For the last half-hour we had been hesitating over a choice of camp-site; we were unable to decide between the valley itself and the shelves of a promontory which dominated it to the east. In the end we settled on the latter because of the tracks left in the snow by séracs which had fallen right from the glacier at the head of the valley.

Alain came back from his trek after water, and his return to camp put an end to my solitary reverie. He had had a look at the lower part of tomorrow's itinerary, and was more full of confidence than ever; the mountain conditions were really good.

It was almost six o'clock, and the sun was sinking towards the Pics des Cavales; the warmth of the day had gone, and an icy breeze got up which set our tent-canvas snapping. In view of the minute size of the candle, begged from a generous grocer, and the weakness of the torch-battery we had been at infinite pains to acquire, we thought it wise to dine before dusk, under the tent. We felt agreeably warm there because of the little spirit-stove, but even that had to be used with extreme parsimony since its fuel was so hard to come by.

Night came gently down, and at seven o'clock all that remained in the sky, behind the Col des Cavales, was a limpid, crystal light, against which the neighbouring crests were silhouetted. One after another the songs of the cascades were silenced. Rolled in a big eiderdown, we thought at first that our two sheepskins made a grand insulation and replaced to advantage the heavy and cumbersome air-mattresses, but in a little while we changed our minds, for a damp cold began to nibble at us in the small of the back and between the shoulder-blades. So much so, that we spent the rest of the long night talking and thinking, without being able to sleep a wink.

But this vigil will remain one of my dearest memories of the mountains. I shall never forget that slow winter evening, at a height of nearly eight thousand feet, in a tight-shut tent with my best friend, so far from all human contact in that gripping silence, and awaiting a struggle of which I had dreamed for ten years. Such peace and quiet make an ideal setting to listen for the " harmony of the spheres," that celestial music of the stars in their eternal courses which according to Pythagoras you may hear when all the sounds of Earth are finally stilled.

About one in the morning I could not resist the temptation to have a look at the weather. The sky was all alive with stars and rich in promise; the cold had become bitter. From that moment onwards, no matter how I tried to restrain it, I began to feel a feverish impatience, an anxious haste to be up and doing. I wanted not so much to start immediately, which would have been senseless folly, as to turn on the clock to the proper moment for departure; I had somehow the secret presentiment that if we meant to snatch the victory tomorrow we should have to cheat ill-fortune by sheer speed. This fever is an old friend of mine; heaven alone knows how many times I have felt it before, as a student facing my examiners, runner waiting for the starter's pistol, and lover longing for the appointed hour of meeting.

Suddenly my thoughts were interrupted by a frightful din; the whole Combe Claire was filled with rumblings, crackings, echoes. An entire block of séracs must have fallen from the glacier, in principle a rare occurrence during the night. Not without some uneasiness, we awaited the end of the terrific bombardment, fearing that one of the projectiles might hit our tent. It was lucky that we had not pitched it in the valley itself, as we had considered the previous evening; it would undoubtedly have been swept away with all its contents. The noise passed, decreased, ceased, and the silence once more took possession of the mountains, immense and crushing.

Six o'clock. This was the long-desired moment when action was to succeed insomnia. We were about to emerge from the tent, make a few paces through the crackling snow, and in the semi-darkness inspect the sky, delicately illumined behind the Pic de Neige Cordier by a translucent dawn . . .

Devil take it ! Contrary to all expectation, the most menacing clouds were driving past before a violent north wind; they were little above our heads. But it was chiefly in the east that the weather threatened. We were utterly dismayed. So despite the favourable promises of yesterday the period of fine days had come to an end at the precise moment when we had most need of them. The change of moon that night had brought us this hateful gift. And from the depths of my puerile distress the words of the Crucified rose to my lips : " My God, My God, why hast Thou forsaken me ? " Despair as excessive as it was sincere, born of our intense fixation on the goal which now seemed likely to escape us.

To assess the situation coolly, there was not one chance in ten that we could succeed in such conditions. So far the weather only threatened, but we should be in a pretty tough spot higher up if it turned really bad. We could visualise only too well the various hardships we should undergo if compelled to retreat by the storm; feeling our way along in a blinding blizzard to the mouth of the valley and the shelf where we were camped; having finally found it, dismantling the tent, half carried-away by the wind, with numbed and painful fingers; clambering down the rocky barrier, hesitatingly, groping for passages altered and made dangerous by fresh snow . . .

Nevertheless we were so desperately set on the expedition that not for an instant did we hesitate about starting. Disregarding our immediate comfort, we would not decide to turn back except in the face of a big storm; we might perhaps climb four-fifths of the way for nothing, but that was a risk we were prepared to accept. We should know how to give up all idea of reaching the summit if prudence so dictated. So perfect was the understanding between us that this compact was sealed without the need of being put into words.

Silently we got ready, just as if the weather had been fine, only seeking to lighten ourselves to the utmost in order to make the greatest possible speed. At 7.15 we left the tent; the weather had worsened and a few flakes were falling. We put on crampons and started off swiftly over favourable snow.

We were soon nearing the snout of the Claire glacier, deeply scored by the fall of séracs during the night. Our path had crossed some day-old tracks which told of the passing of a herd of chamois; their presence so high up at this time of year proved the mildness of the winter of 1943 in the mountains.

A tramp along under the icefall, a short climb over glazed rocks, and we were at the foot of the thousand-foot promontory which, splits the Claire glacier in two. The weather had changed several times since we started; sometimes a fugitive rent in the clouds gave us a glimpse of a scrap of blue sky, at others the most threatening masses came boiling up from the Cavales valley or went rushing through the vast portal of the Col Claire. But the snow had stopped falling. These continual alterations found an echo in me, amplified by my desperate longing; furious hope, mounting anger, resignation and despondency followed on each other's heels, whirling through me like the writhing clouds. I daresay my companion's thoughts were much the same, but we tramped and we tramped as though our bodies had taken charge of us. I must admit that as far as I was concerned the whole ascent was one long ardent prayer for victory; today the crushing problems of a mad world were reduced simply to that for us both.

In spite of the unfavourable conditions we were keeping well up to our time-table; my knowledge of the region, though eleven years old, saved us from making any mistakes in the route, and my friend Alain, iron-willed and steel-muscled, led the way with speed and vigour. We were nearly at the top of the promontory and it was barely nine-thirty, so we decided to call a halt. We had intended to make a meal during this first pause, but such a bitter wind met us from over the Col Claire that our breakfast became a few frugal lumps of sugar.

Then all of a sudden the norther, which had freshened again, managed to get the clouds moving, and in a few moments we found ourselves, to our intense delight, beneath an almost clear sky, looking down at a rippling sea of cloud torn by the neighbouring summits.

" Now nothing can stop us from making it ! " said Alain, not without presumption.

Feverishly we roped up, so as not to let the much-desired opportunity escape, left our rucksacks to lighten ourselves still further, and bundled in our polar equipment attacked our goal, which was now quite close. The snow was deeper, the trail more difficult, and the blizzard was still blowing, sometimes in diaphanous sheets of thinnest gauze, sometimes in fleeting whirlwinds, errant ghosts which died almost at birth. But the cold flung itself upon us in vain; it could not touch us except for our feet, which on several occasions we feared were frost-bitten.

The *rimaye*, to give it its traditional name, was so well-plugged that it did not constitute an obstacle; we climbed a snowbank eight or ten feet high and reached the bottom of the 650-foot couloir which led up to the peak we coveted. After a few pitches we came to a gully where ice made its appearance, but a dozen axe-strokes got the better of it. A little higher up we had to struggle waist-deep in frozen powdery snow. Alain did not hesitate; fed up with trying to make headway in such uncertain footing, he tackled the rocky buttress to the left of the couloir, where we continued our ascent with crampons. There was in general little ice on the rocks, but we had to brush off the covering of snow.

We had not felt the wind since leaving the *rimaye*, protected as we were by the lateral arêtes of the couloir, but we could hear it shrieking furiously above our heads. As we neared the summit ridge the sky began to cloud over again; the powerful thrust of our peak · split the stream flowing before the wind. To the east the Agneaux group and the Pic de Neige Cordier were submerged beneath some menacing grey masses coming up from Les Arves.

Several rather more tricky rock pitches delayed our progress; the fog hid us from one another at rope's length. It was a swift change of scene which could not help but have its effect on us; a phrase from the *Unfinished Symphony* went singing through me like an obsession. A final effort brought us to the summit ridge; from the terrible Cavales face thick wreaths of cloud were billowing up as though out of a crater, but the peak was close by, drawing us irresistibly. In three furious pitches we reached it.

A tremendous peace descended on us, coupled with overflowing joy. I tried to express something of my gratitude to my old friend for the victory he had won yet again for our partnership. · But he had spotted another crest through the mists which might be higher than the one we were on, and, scrupulous in the extreme, decided to take a quick look at it by himself. He unroped and made off along the thread of ruined wall that joined the two peaks, its dizzy slopes plunging down into the fog, and for some minutes I had the feeling of being quite alone, lost in the clouds between earth and sky. The wind had dropped and the cold was less intense; I savoured the precious moments deeply, with a song of thanksgiving in my heart.

Through a rent in the clouds I could see the Lautaret, drowned in blackish mists of the worst description. Suddenly, immaterial, like a pale ghost, white on white between the clouds, there appeared the eastern Meije all powdered with snow; it was the face where our unfortunate friend Voruz had been killed the summer before. The wraith vanished, like a drowned cathedral, engulfed in a new tide of cloud; in its place on the moving screen I saw my own shadow, immense, rainbow-haloed—the Brocken spectre.

Alain, who had made his trip at top speed, was already back, and after a few minutes rest we tore ourselves reluctantly away from the intoxication of the peak to return to earth. The way back was uneventful; swift, united and as rapt as after Holy Communion, we made good use of the traces of our ascent, and soon reached the *rimaye* and the icefall on the Claire glacier. Lower down several delightful glissades brought us, singing at the tops of our voices, to the camp we had left seven hours before in such agony of mind.

Now that the climb was over and our aim achieved, we ceased to be mountaineers and became men again. The sun was shining once more in a clear sky; stretched out in front of the tent, minds completely at rest, we savoured the sensual delights of ease, warmth and satisfied hunger. Before us, still in shadow, the inhuman cliff of La Roche Méane, all roughcast with snow and ice, sliced across the luminous sky and the sun-bathed Cavales glacier. The north wind from which we were sheltered swept this precipice with its mighty breath, dislodging from its flanks and crests long feathery streamers and delicate wisps of powdery snow. Little by little all the Combe des Cavales was filled with these silvery spangles, glittering in the sunlight. And under the strange spell of this music from the heavens we fell silent, listening to the chant of the great wind among the arêtes of La Tour Carrée, Les Jumeaux, Les Clochers . . .

We climbed easily down the rock barrier, put on our skis and flew towards Valfourche over the frozen snow. The sky above us had once more become murky; from the crests of Pic Gaspard heavy masses of cloud were rolling down into the Cavales valley, filling it, blotting it out completely, as a heavy curtain falls across the stage when the play is over. But we cared little for the weather now. By sheer perseverance we were bearing away in our inmost heart a precious sacrament stolen from the mountains, the joy of victory and confidence in ourselves.

On a greatly reduced scale this expedition of ours was a striking replica of the great tragedy through which France was passing. The sky of our motherland was ink-black, like the sky at dawn that morning; the storm-warnings were all too plain to see—the game seemed up. But it was no good losing hope; the best course was to snatch avidly instead, at every favourable sign, and go forward as though in brilliant sunshine. There would be many moments of hope and of despair, but if we stayed united like a cordée through all our trials we should once again find the blue sky and our pride of country and race.

May 1943.

Chapter Six

ON THE NORTH SPUR
OF THE POINTE D'AMONT

The Pointe d'Amont (10,959 feet)
*is one of the four peaks of the Soreiller, situated on the Aiguille du Plat de
la Selle-Plaret chain; it throws out on the Selle slope a splendid spur,
three thousand feet in height, enclosed by the two Diable glaciers. The
first ascent by this route was made in 1932, and was twice repeated, in
1933 and 1942.*

Picture to yourself tall cliffs which leap straight from the pebbles
at their feet to the blue heavens; a jumbled world of arêtes, couloirs,
pinnacles; glaciers nestling against the walls; meadows determined
in spite of snow and rock to climb right to the peaks; valleys
which stretch and probe deep into the heart of the mountains;
that is the Oisans.

For all these things, for its warm light, the hours of happiness
it has given me, the precious memories it has sown broadcast through
my life, I love it with heart and soul. I always considered myself
its spiritual son, and I am happy now to know that it was the cradle
of my forebears. Moreover it is the only great massif exclusively
French, and this is perhaps one more reason why I love it.

There are some valleys in the Oisans whose every feature goes to
create this engaging atmosphere. The Selle valley is one of them, and
so, despite the interminable length of the footpath which leads from

Saint Christophe to the Edouard Bourgeois refuge, it has always given me infinite pleasure to follow it, thinking and dreaming as I go.

Its comfort and solitude and the scenery in which it stands make this cabin one of the most attractive in our Alps. Before it, like the Great Wall of China, the Aiguilles du Soreiller, flanked by the heavy bastions of the Plat de la Selle and the Plaret, shoot up in a single spurt from the two Diable glaciers, the darkness of the ones contrasting violently with the whiteness of the others. Three massive spurs plunge down from the crest towards the Selle valley, thrown off by the Aiguille de Burlan, the Pointe d'Amont and the Plaret; they are quite different in shape, the first being convex, the second concave, while the third forms a long arête on which a slender tower stands like a lighthouse on a digue. Each has its own particular attraction, but the second, built up of magnificent slabs of red-brown granite and hemmed in between two glaciers, is exceptionally tempting. More than just inviting, from the refuge it is sheerly provocative.

As a grateful guest of the little cabin, I had many times felt the challenge of this pure flight of rock. Little by little, it had come to prey unconsciously on my mind like a sweet clinging obsession, and to rid myself of its weight I had to decide to make the climb. You do not always choose your own climbs; sometimes they choose you.

1. First Contact - or Nimrod in spite of himself

July 31st, 1943.

My brother and I were spending a week's holiday at Saint Christophe, going over our beloved massif together. Some easy training-trips up the Bec du Canard and the north arête of Lauranoure had shown us that we were in good shape to tackle greater difficulties. The only trouble was food; rations were an almost insoluble problem, and they were obviously a question of the gravest importance to mountaineers. In spite of this handicap, and the sudden and total disintegration of my footgear, we decided not to remain deaf any longer to the appeal of that tempting spur.

For this trip we agreed to give the refuge a miss and start off from the good beds of the Hôtel des Ecrins. There were several arguments in favour of this solution; a better night, a knowledge of the weather on leaving, simplification of the thorny food problem, a more rational itinerary (the cabin lay above the point of attack) and, let me admit, it also meant I should avoid a long sleepless night full of nervous worry over the coming climb and memories of those killed in the mountains, whose spirits seemed to be wandering about us. Last but not least, thought I, with a touch of superstition, our assault would have that element of surprise which makes the blitzkreig so effective.

It was not yet six o'clock when we left the village behind us and entered the Diable valley, all filled with the dark mystery of night and the murmuring of the torrent. The sky gave no clear indication of what weather we might expect. However, to the west there was a sort of great black hole in the stars—mist, undoubtedly.

Lacking boots, I moved silently along in espadrilles, often stumbling painfully against the stones in the path. My body was still drowsy, but my mind was already reaching out towards our goal. How soon should we see the famous spur which was drawing us on ? Our plan was to cross right over the summit and go down the other side into the Vénéon valley. The dawn came up, all grey. There was the bulging Burlan promontory which our friend Le Ray had climbed for the first time in 1942; just above it appeared the powerful prow of the Pointe d'Amont, our objective.

Our first difficulty was the crossing of the swollen Selle torrent; it was a hard job, particularly in espadrilles, and ended up by my getting an icy footbath, half-willing, half-involuntary. Far from being stimulating, the cold was almost painful to the extremities, and might prove a serious drawback in the succeeding hours. We were now at the base of the arête itself, whose summit stood up against the heavens so high that to see it we had to tilt back our heads. Perhaps it was the effect of my cold bath, but it seemed to me to have a most unwelcoming air about it.

As far as we could remember, the first team to make this climb, Tézenas du Montcel and Dr. Migot, advised attacking the spur from the western Diable glacier, and then using a wide ledge which runs right across the lower wall. This brings you to a height of about 9328 feet, and the start of the real difficulties. Above that we should have to trust to our instinct, for with our usual culpable negligence we had omitted to bring along any precise information on the route.

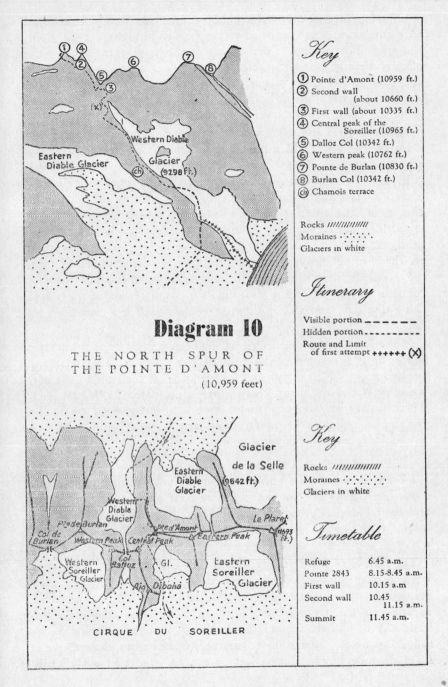

Diagram 10

THE NORTH SPUR OF THE POINTE D'AMONT

(10,959 feet)

Key

① Pointe d'Amont (10959 ft.)
② Second wall (about 10660 ft.)
③ First wall (about 10335 ft.)
④ Central peak of the Soreiller (10965 ft.)
⑤ Dalloz Col (10342 ft.)
⑥ Western peak (10762 ft.)
⑦ Pointe de Burlan (10830 ft.)
⑧ Burlan Col (10342 ft.)
(ch) Chamois terrace

Rocks ////////////
Moraines ·············
Glaciers in white

Itinerary

Visible portion — — — —
Hidden portion - - - - - - -
Route and Limit of first attempt +++++ (X)

Key

Rocks ////////////
Moraines ·············
Glaciers in white

Timetable

Refuge	6.45 a.m.
Pointe 2843	8.15-8.45 a.m.
First wall	10.15 a.m
Second wall	10.45 – 11.15 a.m.
Summit	11.45 a.m.

Up we went, first over stable pebbles, then over long slabs covered with small stones and crowned with a frightful moving scree. Soon the spur shot up into a vertical wall which we skirted along the glacier, already completely clear of snow. André conscientiously cut comfortable steps where, in spite of my soaked espadrilles, I should have felt quite at home if I had not been suffering so much from the cold.

A few pitches and we saw the beginnings of a few ledges on the sides of the spur. Moving alternately over rock and snow we advanced slowly and carefully; the glacier was all split with bluish gulfs, and elsewhere, at the foot of the wall, the holds were slippery and unsafe, being rounded, slanting and covered with pebbles. Moreover, the freezing bath followed by the tramp over ice in espadrilles had completely numbed my feet, which had become dead and clumsy. I do not know whether to lay the blame on that, on the disquieting cliff which stood between us and the summit, the rapid flight of time, or the worsening weather, but the fact remains that I was feeling thoroughly pessimistic about the whole thing that day, and was ready to declare myself beaten before we had really started.

We reached the wide ledge we had seen mentioned, and after following it for some yards began to scale the wall of steep and broken rocks which dominated it. Bearing all the time to the left, we approached the sharp crest which culminated in Pointe 2843. Then, just as we were crossing a gap and about to set foot on the big steps clinging to the eastern flank of the spur, André, who was in the lead, made an imperious sign.

"Ssh! Look!"

I crawled to his side and saw a lovely and unforgettable sight. Less than twenty-five yards away were four chamois, two mothers and their kids; they had been peacefully installed on some of the ledges when they suddenly caught sight of us blocking the only easy outlet.

The little herd was in the grip of unspeakable terror; the females were leaping panic-stricken up and down the steps with the kids pressed close against their flanks. André and I swiftly unroped and approached the troop; their fear increased and they galloped frenziedly to and fro, defying all the laws of balance, leaping gracefully, and madly daring, on to infinitesimal perches close above a sheer drop of three hundred feet or more. And through all this tragic merry-go-round they never once took their eyes off us, the implacably-advancing enemy.

The two mothers tried with all their might to draw their little ones after them towards the gulf, but the babies, though already very clever, could not quite make up their minds to face such a terrain. The sight was so entrancing that we continued, captivated, to approach the unfortunate animals, pushed by I know not what primitive instinct.

" Look out ! " André warned me. " They'll try to get out of this mouse-trap in a minute by charging at us."

Then suddenly all was drama. With a heartbreak at which I could only guess, the two desperate mothers flung themselves head-long over the brink on to the appalling slabs leading down to the glacier in the abyss. It happened in such a flash that I had hardly time to glimpse their flight, or rather their death-defying fall, and their disappearance beneath some projections, a hundred and fifty feet below.

The terrified kids had not dared to follow; one of them was at the end of a ledge only three paces from me. I could hear his tiny hoofs scraping on the granite of the slab to which he had jumped at the very limit of balance; I should have liked to photograph him, but was prevented by his continual movement and my own nervous-ness. Abruptly, risking a fatal fall, he turned and charged along the step between me and the cliff. I shot out my hand instinctively and managed to catch him by the neck as he shot past; behind me my brother let out a yell of delight. Picking the graceful creature up in my arms, I carried it towards the rucksacks we had left at the mouth of the ledge; it was a two-months-old kid weighing at least thirteen pounds. We tried to calm him, for he was panting with fear; by stroking him gently I tried to make him understand my friendship for the animals which live in the mountains.

But my loving gesture and my unaccustomed hand brought him terror rather than peace. In the living flower of his beautiful dark eyes, dilated with anguish, you could clearly read his instinctive horror of us, mankind, though he knew nothing about us. Between us and him " the great barrier " was raised irreparably, and " it had taken our sins piled up through the centuries to make it so solid."

Now that we had him, what were we to do with this kid who was still striving after his lost liberty ? It would be a nice gesture to give him back to his mountains, after a final caress, so that he might perhaps remember that men are not all evil brutes. But he was so young that we doubted whether he could live without his mother, who must surely have been killed in her desperate escape-bid, or had at least fled far away by now. Rather than leave him to perish on this arête, why not take him home alive, to the great joy of my little girls, have him brought up by a goat and give him to the zoological gardens in Grenoble ?

After a lot of hesitation, I decided on this solution and installed him as best I could in my rucksack, without letting him get his head out, since I was afraid of hurting him in the course of the climb which we wanted to carry on with just the same. On the other hand, we left the second little chamois at liberty, though a detour of scarcely thirty feet would have allowed us to capture him.

And so I was cruel enough to carry off this kid from her who made him and from the mountains he loved. This despite the fact that I understood all his passion for freedom, all the sorrow of a mother for a lost child; a vision of my own two little ones had even passed fleetingly across my mind. But I failed to make the necessary gesture; in the end, I turned out to be no better than the rest of them.

Returning to the original aim of the trip, we climbed towards the first slabs of the wall. My rucksack was now weighed down not only with the kid but with my axe, which was useless from there on; we had come to the splendid granite, solid, homogeneous, massive, where climbing was pure joy and perfectly safe despite the stiffening of the slope. Above these slabs, a fine double fissure led to a balcony overlooking the abyss on the western side. More slabs and steps followed; up to that point the route was plain, and we had practically no hesitations. Higher up, the wall steepened again ; should we continue by the arête as heretofore, or cast about for the weak spot in the obstacle? A ledge led attractively away towards the eastern slope, but the cliff overhung to such an extent that it was impossible to stand upright on it; you had to crawl along on your forearms, body dangling above the void. A memory of the Grépon made me call it the " Râteau de Chèvre."

Beyond, this ledge continued easily for about sixty yards as far as a couloir paved with enormous slabs; however, something told me not to follow this obvious route, inviting as it was. A direct climb a little beyond the Râteau de Chèvre did in fact bring us to a zone of terraces dominated by the pediment of the cliff, which pierced the sky three hundred feet above. The slabs of tawny granite which separated us from it, shortened by the perspective, were of striking beauty but looked like being extraordinarily hard to climb.

My little boarder had not become resigned to his captivity for a single moment; he fought frenziedly all the time. His abrupt movements often caused a certain upset in the style and safety of my climbing; André, laughing as he belayed me, remarked several times on the peculiar malformations occasioned to my rucksack by the kid's capers—he kicked like a child in its mother's womb. Despite this handicap I was extremely anxious to make a success of the trip; it would certainly be something out of the ordinary under such conditions !

Instead of tackling the main cliff, we decided to see what a turning movement would do. To the west it was hopeless, since the terrace ended in a formidable gulf, but to the south-east, on the other hand, a broken ledge led towards a most attractive shoulder. Obviously that was the place to attack without further delay. To reach this first objective, a step ten to twelve feet in height between two ledges compelled us to make a nasty passage at full stretch, body hanging over an impressive sheer drop.

But a sharp disappointment awaited us at the shoulder; beyond it there was only a wide-mouthed couloir built of very steep slabs, while above it golden rock soared up hopelessly towards an over-hang. Without any real conviction, but simply for conscience' sake, André climbed up a few yards, then I heard him declare that that was not the way, and back he came with some difficulty to where I stood. We should have to try elsewhere. We returned slowly along the ledges, making a short rappel at the bad spot for safety.

A fresh examination of the wall from the terrace brought us to the conclusion that the attack direct, though very exposed, stood a good chance of success. So we climbed first to the base of a gendarme, braced against the arête as though cowering timidly there, and after placing a piton, made our way up the first pitch of the cliff. The ascent was not only difficult but very impressive, the face being almost vertical. I rejoined André on a platform so narrow that on my arrival he had to climb up a couple of yards in order that I might settle myself with the smallest degree of stability. The slabs above shot up again, steeper than ever.

In this airy and uncertain situation we started a discussion on what was to be done; my little chamois participated with a series of violent contortions that almost overbalanced me.   After an objective review of the position, we finally resigned ourselves to retreating; we were too heavily laden and had too few pitons to tackle the great wall, besides which it was already two o'clock and the weather was beginning to look distinctly threatening.   Bitterness descended heavily on the party.   We estimated that we must have reached a height of about ten thousand feet, which meant that from the spot where we found the chamois we had only climbed around six hundred feet in nearly three hours, a pace so mediocre that it had inevitably condemned us to failure.

Joylessly we retraced our steps down the pitches we had climbed with so much hope.   My clandestine traveller continued to make unexpected bounds; he certainly thought very little of this sort of climbing.   His annoyance must have been extreme, for now he was bleating faintly.

"Poor little mountain fawn !   Just be patient for a few more minutes.   We're going back to where we caught you, like criminals returning to the scene of the crime.   Then I'll open the sack so that you can get some fresh air and take a last look at the heights where you were born."

The cordée slid down the last slabs to the wide ledges of the Pointe 2843 level.

"Open the bag, quick !   The kid's stopped moving ; perhaps he's calmed down.   What's he doing head down like this, though ? "

Alas, it was nothing but a tiny corpse I drew from my rucksack. The poor little chamois was dead ; no doubt he was rendering up his gentle soul to the God of Beasts when he bleated a few moments before.   In his struggles he must, unbeknown to me, have turned himself upside down and stayed that way for a long time till he suffocated.

I was dumbfounded, tortured with regret and remorse as though I had committed a deadly sin.   So this was the evil I had done, I, who called myself the friend of the chamois and inveighed against those who hunted them.   This day had been a decided failure from every point of view.   The second kid, either terrified by what had happened to his cousin or incapable of finding his way, was still vainly awaiting his mother in the same place.   We had only to stretch out our hand to take him from the narrow balcony where he was perched, but it was enough to have one murder on our conscience ; we left him to his fate.

We threw a last look at the superb cliff which had rebuffed us, and then fled down into the valley like the thieves we were. Shaky holds, unstable pebbles, unpleasant glacier, crumbling moraines, polished slabs, great screes; all the disagreeable passages of the morning followed one another in reverse order. We had not thought to see them again. Then the path was unrolling before us, and soothed by the even pace I wrapped myself in my dreams, which took me back in thought on to the enticing spur.

Today we had given up the struggle about three hundred feet below the summit of the great wall. After those pitches, which were certainly the most difficult, a much less arduous climb must take you to the top in an hour at the most, by way of a second calmer rise and a third which was practically good-natured. The insidious desire to pull off the victory we had missed was already laying siege to my subconscious, taking possession little by little and imposing itself; I made up my mind that we simply had to come back in force and in better form to wipe out such a defeat.

Now, instead of success and a graceful live kid, we were bringing home something which would entail endless reports; hunting an under-age animal during the close season and without permits, in territory controlled by the Eaux et Forêts . . . Fortunately the law, which is tolerant no matter what may be said of it, has decreed that such an infraction is only penalised when one is caught red-handed. Otherwise I should never have dared write this story, but I daresay you would not have missed much !

2. Conquest

September 5th, 1943.

The idea of going back had implanted itself so firmly in my mind that forty days later I started off with four companions to cycle to Saint Christophe in dazzling sunshine. André, despite the difficulties of travelling, had come from Toulon expressly for the climb, while my friend Le Ray and Jean Berthet, one of the finest mountaineers in Grenoble, had also agreed to make the attempt with us. I had given them an enthusiastic description of the airy route which had remained an *Unfinished Symphony* for us. Alain's brother-in-law, the young Jean Mauriac, was a recent convert to climbing, and would accompany the party as far as the refuge so that he might have the revelation of the celestial nights of the high mountains.

Standing before the cabin in the falling dusk, we enthusiastically scrutinised the lovely spur whose manifold details were revealed by the last rays of sunshine. The rocky spires of the arête were still ablaze long after the foot of it was submerged in the nocturnal tide. Round the table, in the congenial warmth of friendship, we rapidly made a plan of campaign. The candle was blown out early. Thinking of those endless slabs of red-brown granite with their fine solid holds, I slipped gently into a deep sleep, lulled by the murmur of the wind and the thousand tiny noises you hear by night in a refuge . . .

Half-past five. It was still dark, but the sky was already paling behind the Plaret. A great draught of cold air helped to rouse bodies and minds, and less than an hour later we were all ready.

Jean Mauriac assisted rather enviously with our preparations for departure. He no longer regarded us in the same light as yesterday; we were no longer companions to him, the ardent neophyte, but those who were about to have revealed to them a mystery from which he was still excluded. I understood his thoughts without his saying a word; they had been mine as a child, when, gambolling under my mother's eye in the alpine meadows that were the very frontier of the forbidden garden of the heights, I respectfully watched the mountaineers who came back from it, haloed in my sight by their initiation into that magical world which even then I so passionately desired.

The trip began with an annoying descent of almost five hundred feet; from the torrent a rapid crossing of the moraines brought us to the base of the spur itself. Instead of skirting it to the west, as on the previous occasion, we discovered that we could get up to the footing of the wall by means of some easy chimneys in the middle of some grassy slabs. In a little while we reached the western Diable glacier, having missed all the unpleasant passages of our last approach. The cordées were made up, I going with Alain and André with Berthet; today the honour was not to the family.

Without axes, but with the aid of hammers for those who had them, we clambered up the glacier, which had changed prodigiously in a month; its level had sunk by at least six feet, and the crevasses and *rotures* had opened so inordinately wide that it looked as though it was going to be pretty hard to get on to the spur itself. Ropes taut, we approached the rocks, from which the glacier was widely separated.

Alain, reaching the extreme edge by careful crawling, informed us that we were all four on a huge sheet of ice overhanging an abyss; at that precise moment a sharp crack like a pistol-shot resounded through the air, and we had the fleeting impression that all the portion of the glacier beneath our feet had subsided several inches. This warning of what might so easily have been a catastrophe encouraged us to leave that unhealthy spot and make a very wide detour across the glacier to gain the big ledge from above.

A rapid climb gave access to the steps of Pointe 2843, scene of our hunt whose vicissitudes I explained to Alain and Berthet. There was no sign of chamois that day, only a cold wind inviting us to action without delay. We started happily upwards and swiftly covered the familiar pitches; the whole party was in fact impatient to get to the real difficulties. It was barely nine o'clock when we reached the shelves, three hundred feet below the summit of the great wall, which more or less formed the limit of the previous attempt. There it became essential to exchange boots for espadrilles, an operation which would notably increase the weight of the seconds' rucksacks.

While we were all busy, André discovered unmistakable and fairly fresh signs that a chamois had passed that way. Why and how such an incursion on its part ? What extraordinary motive could have driven the animal up to this airy terrace ? André and I looked at each other like accomplices, the memory of the stolen kid going through our minds. Here was proof positive that our captive's loving mother, having watched from afar the carrying off of her little one and our flight towards the peak, had tried with all her might to follow the trail of her baby's ravishers. To do this she must no doubt have managed to get around certain pitches of our route by climbing some huge continuous slabs to the left which were better suited to her means. But God knows what mortal difficulties she must have faced, spurred on by wounded mother-love. A fresh wave of remorse went over me.

While we were talking about it, Alain the realist was making a close inspection of the wall which dominated us. His mind was made up; rejecting my suggestion for a direct attack such as we had tried a month earlier, he proposed that we tackle the eastern flank of the spur from the shoulder, which appealed to him just as irresistibly as it had to us at the end of July. So we decided to have another look at the possibilities of that route.

The cordées reached the platform in a few minutes, crossing with great dash the gap in the ledges which gave access to it. Despite the pessimistic remarks of André, who had unpleasant memories of his previous attempt on these slabs, Alain climbed the first above the jumping-off place. I belayed him carefully, the rope running smoothly over my shoulder. My partner mounted quietly and neatly, and I could no longer see anything of him but his soles; his slow flowing movements were aimed at not disturbing a balance which seemed to depend solely on adhesion. He let fall a few monosyllables expressing his optimism and joy to the rest of us, crowded together on the terrace, heads in air; then the rope stopped.

" Come on ! You're sumptuously belayed ! "

What marvellous and all-too-short minutes those were, spent in intimate possession of that wall springing from the abyss; I recall them as a moment of intense happiness. It was a climb as harmonious as a melody, light as a dance, a glimpse of a mountaineer's paradise. The body moved up without effort, as though released from the force of gravity; delicately brushing the wall, its weight went in turn from toe-tip to toe-tip. As the pull of one arm died, the other came into action; a hold appeared each time you wanted it, true, strong and welcoming. It was like strumming on a piano, softly and caressingly; it was all smooth-flowing movement in a closer and closer union with the rock. There was no roughness, no tension, no anxiety or hesitation; nothing but balance, gentleness and subtlety. It is on such pitches that you savour in all its strength the art of climbing, and taste a pleasure which is not merely physical and sporting, but intellectual as well, for like good music or a great play it reaches the soul through the body.

Alain was awaiting me on top of a rocky little balcony, his face one big beam of delight; even before I reached him our coryphæus, impatient for action, was already off again up some new slabs. The dance he was leading took him, by way of a stylish traverse, towards a vertical and widely-gaping furrow in the cliff; he scaled it with sureness and speed as far as a zone of terraces. I had an absolute conviction that today my friend could neither hesitate nor make a mistake, and least of all fall; his ascent was a triumph. I was bathed in happiness, calm and soothing; he alone could give me such confidence in myself in the mountains. However, I was not the only one who was conscious of intense joy; did I not hear one of my companions muttering rapturously from the bottom of his heart as he scaled those marvellous slabs of granite: " You know, I think this is really better than making love ! And yet . . . ! "

But the cliff above, arched into an overhang, repulsed us; we had to cast about. To the left, enormous flawless slabs opposed all progress, but to the right, on the contrary, an attractive ledge ran between two walls, narrowing all the way, as far as a fairly steep bit of ridge, behind which it disappeared. There was nothing for it but to follow this route laid out across the mountain. Alain advanced to the corner-stone, studied the problem set by the following pitch, and called me up to him to help with a traverse which he described as very tricky. As I made my way along the little ledge, I caught glimpses straight down between my legs of the second cordée, which was having fun with the granite slabs eighty feet below. In perfect safety myself, I nevertheless got a vivid impression of height and space.

I belayed my companion round a splinter of rock while he tackled one of those places on the other side of the crest which mountaineers call a " ticklish bit." The ledge stopped for about six feet at the angle of the crest and then began again; to make the traverse still more sporting, the cliff bulged at this point, just enough to push you outwards. Taking delicate purchase on infinitesimal holds, which were unusual for this spur in being very friable, you had to descend lightly a trifle below the break in the ledge, negotiate the " nose " of the arête without overbalancing, reach out, stretch yourself, stretch yourself still further, and grasp the edge of the new shelf with your fingertips.

We played the tightrope-walker one after the other with slow and calculated movements, and soon the team was reunited on a comfortable terrace at the foot of a face about 150 feet in height placed on the very crest of the spur, halfway up the great wall. It looked like providing an extremely airy and pretty exciting climb, though inferior to the preceding pitches. After noting this and tracing a possible itinerary, we decided to rest for a few minutes to allow the second cordée to catch up.

The weather was still superb; despite the season, a real summer sun blazed down on the rocks. Towards the west, beyond the gulf carved out by the Diable glacier, rose the massive Burlan spur, parallel to the one we were climbing. Alain pointed out the new route he had found up it the year before; I was unable to accompany him at the time, and it will always remain one of my keenest regrets. Eastward, the crests of the Plaret and its satellites stood up against the light; long shafts of sunshine streamed through their battlements down to the depths where the glaciers lay purring under their caresses. In the background La Meije, haughtier than ever, lifting herself above the Têtes du Replat, seemed to ask us, "Am I not still the loveliest of all?" At our feet the Amont spur plunged from fall to fall like a frozen cascade; from above the pitches we had climbed were so distorted by the perspective as to be scarcely recognisable. Not far from its base I could make out the Selle refuge, cowering at the bottom of the abyss.

Up here you could fill your lungs with the peace and liberty of the mountains. Today, in the joy of action and the feeling of well-being which comes with success, we had completely forgotten that down below, far away, the fate of the world gone mad was being decided, along with that of our country, by savage slaughter. We scarcely knew whether we should be ashamed or glad of our own inaction in the midst of chaos.

(Let me say here and now that the word "inaction" should not be taken too literally. Metropolitan France was certainly officially out of the war at that time, but many of her sons were participating in that underground work which hastened our liberation. And one of us, Le Ray, was already at the head of the armed Resistance in the Isère).

Doubtless our hour would come. Meanwhile we were deeply appreciative of the immense serenity of this valley, the pure air and the blue sky. A spontaneous song of thanksgiving to the Most High welled up in me without stint, for the sheer happiness He gave me thereby. No cathedral can ever lift my soul half as well as the temple of the mountains; it is there that the most ardent prayers rise without end from my heart.

The second cordée arrived, beaming with pleasure over the pitches they had just climbed, and off we went for fresh aerial struggles. A short pitch in the very middle of the face, followed by a quite tricky traverse to just beyond its right edge, and we were at the foot of a tall wide chimney. Alain speeded up his climb, sensing that he was about to master the great wall; the rope flew up behind him, and a shout of delight told me that he had reached the top. I joined him without delay, gathering a few last airy impressions on the way; from now on the difficulties were behind us, even though there remained a climb of over six hundred feet to the peak.

The point we had reached was prolonged by an extremely airy arête, a regular ruined wall between two gulfs, to the foot of a sharp-edged abrupt gendarme between a hundred and a hundred-and-thirty feet in height. From all appearances, it was best to skirt its western flank by descending two or three pitches. While we were executing this manoeuvre promptly and with ease, Alain, either from laziness, whimsy, or the desire to save himself a few yards, got on to some very slippery slabs, and had to face both trouble and our friendly mockery.

The second wall awaited us, but it proved simple enough. The rock continued excellent, and the climb became nothing more than an agreeable form of gymnastics, thanks to the superabundant holds, so it took the party only half-an-hour to make an end of it. At the top we awarded ourselves the lunch-hour which our appetites were demanding so imperiously. Between the mouthfuls we had nothing but praise for the trip, the quality of the climb, the view, the fine weather and the friendly atmosphere of the whole expedition. United in a true alpine brotherhood, the cordées formed a team in which each was conscious not only of his own strength, but of that of all the others; you can tackle Nature with safety and confidence under such conditions.

And now, to bring our trip to a conclusion, we had only to scale the last three hundred feet which separated us from the Pointe d'Amont. The boots, which were not intended simply to weight our rucksacks, came into their own again here. After a few steps we got into a zone of frightfully split grey rocks, so to avoid knocking each other about, the two parties decided to follow different routes and approach the peak by opposite arêtes. Alain and I chose the eastern one, and our companions therefore went off to the western side to take the normal path to this little-frequented summit.

Our ascent was carried on to the accompaniment of a noisy cannonade of rolling stones. One good-sized and extremely angular lump missed me by little; in revenge, and so that its time should not be quite wasted, it got its own back by inflicting a deep cut on the hand that had dared to deflect it, so I blazed our trail willy-nilly.

At last we were at the foot of the arête, up which a climb of fifty feet would bring us to the summit. Here I was reminded of a traverse made eleven years before from the eastern to the central peak of the Soreiller via the Pointe d'Amont. An accident which nearly proved fatal had cut the hands of my companions to the quick, and the ascent of this last section of the arête beneath the summit had been hard work with our cripples. It was not going to be any too easy today either, in nailed boots and with my hand streaming with blood; Alain, who had cleared the obstacle, had, I admit, to hang on to the rope in real earnest while I struggled up as best I could. And we rejoined our two companions on the summit, where they had arrived some minutes before. It was not yet noon.

We decided on a long halt. To get the full flavour out of hours spent in action and strife, it is essential to relax completely on the peak they have won for you. Such is the dreamless sleep of warriors after battle. Today had been heaven on earth for us; the conditions of our climb had been ideal. We had really had a dream-trip, one which held nothing but joy, beauty and harmony, with anguish, disappointment and suffering severely banished. Now, in the silence of the heights beneath the radiant sun, we took communion in peace and gladness.

It mattered little that to get back to Grenoble we had still to descend a crumbling precipice to the Soreiller valley (filled for us with memories of our youth) walk five miles from Les Etages to Saint Christophe, and then have nothing but our bicycles to carry us home. We were taking with us a happiness so shining that nothing could tarnish it. Once this lovely sunlit trip was over, despite the difficulties of the return, the fatigue in our muscles, despite the sadness of the dark hours of after-the-war, our distress over the fate of our country, despite everything, the joy would remain in our souls, an inexhaustible source of hope and strength.

October—November, 1943.

Chapter Seven

EDGINGS

The two stories which follow should really find no place in this little book, since they treat of climbs made not in the Oisans, but in secondary neighbouring massifs. Just the same I have put them in. When you are trying to make a flower-garden, borders are not to be despised. For those who may take this comparison amiss, let me add that the sensations I experienced during the course of these two climbs were quite as intense, and sometimes even more so, than those I have felt in many true high-mountain trips.

1. A Night on the Moucherotte (6,221 feet)

October 3rd, 1932.

A summit of the Vercors overlooking Grenoble, which can be reached in a couple of hours from Saint Nizier by means of a footpath, but whose dizzy eastern face, soaring twelve or thirteen hundred feet above the Forges valley, had apparently not been climbed more than three times at this date.

It was on October 2nd, 1932, that Alain, Jacques and André succeeded in making the first ascent of the east face of the Dibona, a project they had had in mind for several years. The enterprise had taken only two out of the three days set aside for it, so the team, anxious to make full use of the last day before Alain's departure, and having bested the granite cliff which had disturbed their sleep for so long, thought that they would like to try their skill on a difficult limestone wall.   The leader, a disciple of the Kaisergebirge school, wanted in fact to take his cordée up the east face of the Moucherotte.   Plossu had blazed a trail up this scarp some ten or more years before, but they were pretty sure that nobody had followed in his footsteps. (Actually two other parties had also made the dangerous climb).

After their victory of the previous day, it seemed a very slight undertaking to the three companions.   Tired by yesterday's exertions, they rose late, and perhaps a little drunk with success, never even bothered to turn up in the Alpine reviews any information there might be about the intended climb.   Estimating lightly that the whole thing would not take more than a couple of hours, they drove cheerfully off at last somewhat after noon, having completely forgotten that since the day before, while they were up in the Oisans, winter time had come into force.

Two o'clock.   In espadrilles, with pitons and karabiners clinking merrily at their waists, the companions left the car parked, ominously, against the wall of the graveyard at Saint Nizier.   A steep track struck up into the forest, and Alain, as they tramped along, told his friends about the various limestone climbs he had made around Garmisch.   Soon they were in the Forges valley, a deep fold which died at the foot of the wall they were making for, just as the long Atlantic swell breaks against the Breton cliffs.   They hurried towards it head in air, studying the best route to take; a series of chimneys and cracks looked promising, though the outlet above was somewhat uncertain.   Still, that was of little consequence.   Someone else had done it; they could do it too.   It was three o'clock; before five they would have gained the summit.

There were steep slopes of grass near the bottom of the wall, on which their espadrilles skidded.   The three were wiping their feet on the mat like well-bred people before entering the domain of their host, the Moucherotte, an enchanted garden which was to detain them for almost fifteen hours, nearly eight times as long as they had foreseen.

The low grey sky hung like a lid over the Grésivaudan; mists swirled untidily about the topmost point, but again, no matter.   By five o'clock they would be on their way via the peak down the path through the underbrush.

Alain attacked the first chimney of damp and friable rock. It appeared right away that there were going to be serious difficulties; actually, one only became aware of their nature after embarking on pitches which, owing to the illusion peculiar to limestone climbs, had seemed perfectly practicable from below. Hammers came into play at once, and the clang of driven pitons echoed in the stillness; the sound rose till it was like a clear song telling of the iron piercing the heart of the stone.

Slowly the rope went up behind the leader, who climbed calmly enough, clinging by toe and finger-tips, but with every nerve tense. His usual reliability was severely tested for some minutes by the appalling character of the rock, but finally, having crossed a second very steep grassy shelf, he hoisted himself at full rope's length into a little grotto where Jacques and André, their enthusiasm considerably damped by the first three hundred feet, joined him one after the other.

What remained of the climb was extremely confused: a crazy wall built up of a mass of buttresses, overhangs, cracks and pinnacles, sprinkled with fir-trees leaning romantically over the abyss. And a stubborn vegetation struggled for life wherever it could, to the great detriment of the purity of the rock-climb as such.

More grass-belts, then at last a zone of real solid rock, the only one of the trip. The three could hardly believe their luck in being able to make use, even for a few yards, of good safe holds from which they could swing without the slightest trepidation. But their joy was of short duration; why was the sky getting dark so early ? The day seemed to be on the wane, and the light along the crest was dim and smoky. They looked at their watches. Five o'clock and twilight already ? Lord, they had forgotten that cursed change of time. The pessimist of the party began croaking at once, and talked of beating a retreat with all possible speed by rappelling down the way they had come.

"Out of the question," said Alain flatly. "It would take longer than going up. The top can't be far off, and anyway we shan't be shinning up those beastly vertical chimneys; we can take this nice little rising ledge."

At the end of the narrow shelf was a cairn built of a few stones; Jacques, in passing, found in it the card of Zwingelstein—mountain

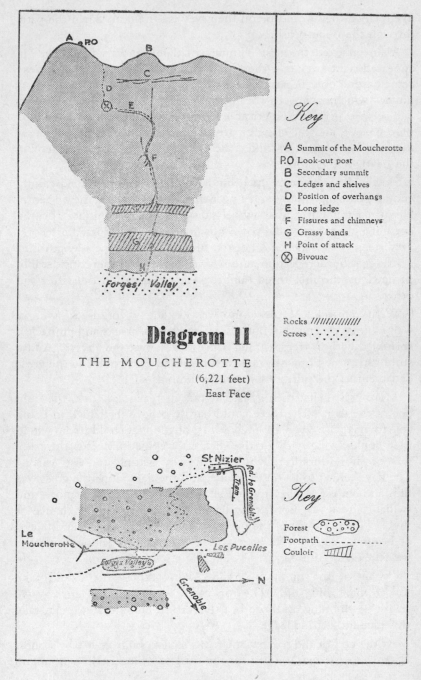

Diagram II

THE MOUCHEROTTE
(6,221 feet)
East Face

Key

A Summit of the Moucherotte
P.O Look-out post
B Secondary summit
C Ledges and shelves
D Position of overhangs
E Long ledge
F Fissures and chimneys
G Grassy bands
H Point of attack
⊗ Bivouac

Rocks //////////////
Screes ·.·.·.·.·.

Key

Forest
Footpath ------------
Couloir

vagabond—who had come that way in 1930. The cordée continued along the tiny cornice, which overlooked an abyss of rounded and glassy slabs; a slip by one of the climbers during this exposed but by no means difficult traverse would be a disaster. Pitons ? They had no time to spare for those; it was a fight against time with the advancing night.

The continuation of the minute ledge brought them up against a face of flaky limestone, all broken and cracked. The end was in sight; the summit could hardly be far away—it only remained for the cordée to surmount this last obstacle. Then they could stroll peacefully back through the forest and drive home, talking as they went; the family would be there to welcome them, they would have a good meal and a quiet evening and finally drift off into a sound sleep still thinking of the day's triumph—all on condition they cleared these last few yards.

Alain tackled the face with a will. In pitch darkness, unable to use a single piton, he tested the rotten stone in search of firm holds, and his progress was slow in the extreme. Time and time again the rock broke away with a sharp crack and imperilled his balance, which was precarious at best. His two companions, side by side on a tiny shelf and almost without means of belaying the party, followed his efforts anxiously by the rope and his white espadrilles, which were all they could vaguely glimpse through the murk. Alain battled furiously for nearly half-an-hour, but in vain; the top of the face overhung a trifle and defeated all his attacks. After a number of fruitless attempts he had to confess himself beaten.

" Can't do a thing without seeing."

Then somehow or another he had to climb down the few yards so laboriously gained, which involved more long minutes of groping, always on the verge of overbalancing and in the fear that something might give under his weight. Bit by bit the white espadrilles came back through the gloom to Jacques and André, and finally the three friends were reunited at the end of the narrow gutter. The night was by now so thick that there could be no further question of moving. Faced with the prospect of a delightful bivouac, each of them reacted according to temperament.

" Here's a rum go," thought Alain the adventurous.

" Pretty uncomfortable," sighed André the sybarite.

" It would be a lot funnier if our people weren't expecting us back," reflected the anxious Jacques. A trifle pale about the gills, he laughed nervously, choking down the useless reproach which had risen to his lips, " If only you'd listened to me—" and gave the rock a spiteful punch, though it was not to blame.

Without doing any crying over spilt milk, all three of them felt that their position was not exactly conspicuous for its brilliance; they were simply clinging to the top of a great slab by fingers and toes. Bivouac they must, but where ? They could no more think of staying where they were all night than they could of retracing their steps, in complete darkness, over that long exposed traverse to the shelf with the cairn. What was to be done ? Peering about through the gloom, one of them thought he could see a slight fold in the rock, a couple of yards further down the slab, and a laborious descent that far confirmed the hypothesis.

" Well, with time and patience we may be able to make something of it."

The first step was for everyone to assure his own safety with a well-placed piton, leaving just enough rope to allow him to reach the scene of operations. Hammers and the remaining pitons were vigorously plied; at the end of his cord each man battered, broke and levelled. Haste was absolutely forbidden. In the first place it was impossible to see what they were doing, which naturally cut down their speed; secondly, they had plenty of time—at least thirteen hours to kill; and finally, the movement would help to keep them warm. Further, in order that subjects of conversation which could be well chewed over in the course of the night might not be wasted, there must be no skipping from one to another until the first had been thoroughly exhausted.

After two hours of this forced labour, the three had contrived to chisel out the beginnings of a little gutter to take the end of their behinds and a notch where they could wedge their heels; despite all the care they had lavished on the job, it was still hardly seven o'clock. Nothing remained but to move in, which was soon done. They hung there on the very knife-edge between balance and falling; only the ropes held them to their giddy perch. Without those it could have been simply a matter of minutes before they went toppling down into the chasm below.

Suddenly the cold seized them, for with admirable foresight two of them had seen fit to wear only miserable sleeveless pullovers, and the third a thin cotton jacket. At first it was nothing but a slight shiver running down the spine, accompanied by a vague feeling of discomfort, but little by little the sensation became localised and their lower jaws set up an unceasing chatter. True, by way of compensation, the climbers had an illuminated map of Grenoble spread out before them, twinkling with a thousand lights at the bottom of the gulf over which they were suspended. For some minutes they played an absorbing game, identifying streets and squares and the house where by now they should have been snug and warm (and where no doubt the family was already getting a trifle worried).

But the cold, momentarily forgotten, continued to seep into their bodies, along with a new torment—hunger. It was in fact dinner-time, when they should have been seated at a laden table engaged in recuperating their strength. A careful search of the only haversack brought to light their sole provision, a lemon. No, thanks; nobody had the courage to touch it.

So to cheat the cold and hunger, the weather and their general discomfort, they began to sing. They ran through all their repertoire, twice, three times over; marching songs, carabineer songs, hymns, psalms. After a particularly successful Ave Maria they tried to picture the reactions of a casual stroller or a belated hunter, down below on the Forges footpath, on hearing these songs drifting down from Heaven through the night.

But the double torment, driven away for a few minutes by the music, came back to gnaw at them more fiercely than ever. All right, they knew how to fool it; they would neutralise the evils of cold and hunger by the Coué system. So, solemnly and fervently, they tried to persuade themselves that they were seated at a table covered with delicate dishes which they proceeded to describe at great length; afterwards they went to a show in an overheated theatre, (a lovely way to spend an evening) then home again to slip into their downy beds and pull the warm covers right up to the chin— like this . . . A brief interlude while the results of the process were being analysed. Then,

"Oh, nuts. Let's talk about something else; the system's no good. The cold certainly got the best of that."

A silence fell, the first since the start of the bivouac. In the still air the Seyssins clock tower broadcast ten strokes.

"Heck, I thought it was midnight at least."

By now they were all three curled up as tight as possible, eyes fixed on Grenoble; the sight of it, so near and yet so far, was a regular Trial of Tantalus. And there, down in the city, appeared a lighted caterpillar which wriggled its way off towards the west.

" My train ! " sighed Alain, suddenly remembering his intended departure for Paris that very evening.

Still eight hours to hold out. Heaven send that the rain which was beginning to threaten would hold off. The three companions in misfortune carried on as best they could; they told all their stocks of "good stories," padding them out to enormous proportions. But little by little the breeze and the cold stone numbed their thinly-clad bodies and deadened their tired spirits. The silences became longer and more frequent . . .

Let us leave them to their troubles and go back, so that we can watch this little Alpine drama from the other side of the curtain, with the waiting family.

In their flat in Grenoble, Jacques' and André's parents were not worrying—yet—about their sons' lateness. Mother had hardly begun to remark on it.

" They ought to be back by now."

" They won't be long," said her husband reassuringly.

Twenty-past eight. Still no sign of them. The cold hand of fear touched Mother's loving heart; she scarcely tasted her dinner when they finally decided to have it by themselves.

" We must phone Saint Nizier and find out."

" The little Renault," reported the postmistress, who had agreed to go and make enquiries in the village, " is still parked by the graveyard."

The delay began to have an ugly look.

Time passed. To lend each other countenance, the parents pretended to be busy, one with some odd jobs, the other reading, but their thoughts were elsewhere. It must have been presentiment; the " children " had been on dozens of trips and it was no new thing for them to be late returning, but somehow they had never felt as they did tonight. Besides, it was tempting Providence too far; yesterday they had tackled the great virgin face of the Dibona, today they were assaulting that sheer limestone wall—a pitcher can go to the well once too often.

The clock struck nine. They called the Saint Nizier postmistress again and received the same reply.

"The car is still there."

By now there could be no room for doubt; there must have been an . . . accident. It is a word you scarcely dare say when it touches you personally. That very night, as it happened, there was a meeting of the Alpine Club committee; quick, telephone and ask their advice, and, since one must, their help.

The opinions given were markedly pessimistic.

"Any idea of a bivouac on a climb like that can be ruled out right away. I'm afraid one must expect the worst."

As for help, they offered that at once with great alacrity. Good mountaineers who volunteered their services were immediately enlisted, and a rendezvous was arranged for ten o'clock. This ready assistance did something to relieve the distress of the poor parents, which was rapidly becoming more than they could bear. As fast as possible, feeling that their sons' lives might perhaps depend on the loss of a minute, they changed, stuffed medicaments, food and clothing into Tyrolean bags, and went down to get their car, only to find it right at the back of the garage, from which, in the attendant's absence, they had to manhandle over twenty others which were blocking the way, a task that taxed them to the utmost.

Ready at last, the search-party shot off along the road to Saint Nizier. Nobody spoke; the rescuers dozed, Father, trying not to show how stricken he was, concentrated on getting the last ounce of speed out of the car, while poor Mother, past caring who saw, no longer made any attempt to restrain her flood of tears.

"You bring up your two boys with so much love and care and ambition—you move to the mountains so that they can draw strength and inspiration from them—and it all ends like this—mangled bodies at the foot of a cliff . . ."

Half-past eleven at Saint Nizier; an ink-black night, spitting with rain. Jacques' car was still parked by the graveyard wall. They started quickly off up the Moucherotte footpath; Mother's memories of her sons walked with her, little boys, big boys, and finally young men.

"I should never have let them learn to love these mountains. Now they've taken them from me forever. Oh, God, let them be only hurt . . . perhaps with a little luck . . . but what's the good of trying to fool yourself ?"

So the unhappy parents, bowed beneath their cross, went to their Calvary through the forest, at once feverishly impatient and terrified of learning their children's fate. The pace was fast—ever faster.

"A hæmorrhage stopped in time might not be fatal."

In the darkness the trunks of the huge firs seemed to be circling about the lanterns.

"But look at the difficulty of finding the bodies on a night like this."

Father tense, and Mother with tear-stained face, climbed side by side to meet their misfortune.

One o'clock in the morning. Up in the Forges valley the party swung away to the left from the Moucherotte footpath; they would soon reach the base of the murderous wall and the search for the vanished climbers would get under way. A keen wind was sweeping the valley; the clouds felt low overhead and it was drizzling. Without much hope, the caravan sent a long call pealing up the enigmatic black cliff-face veiled in darkness.

"Où où où où où . . ."

With a flourish the breeze flung itself on the shouts and carried them off, heaven knows where. For seconds that seemed an age there was nothing but silence, a silence so heavy that its weight hung crushing on them all. It certainly did not look as though there would be any answer.

Then suddenly, while the rescuers waited, straining their ears, there came a sound from the mountain, muffled and indistinct, so like the original call that it might almost have been its far-off echo.

"Où où où où où . . ."

They hesitated, wondering whether they could be mistaken, but Mother's sure instinct had recognised her children's voices. For her the nightmare was over, and happiness came back in a flood; she clung trembling to her companion's arm as she whispered, "Thank God, they're alive."

They started shouting again, and answers came back each time from the cliff, but the words, distorted by the wind, were not at all clear. However, the rescuers thought they understood the lost party to say that they had been benighted not far from the summit, but were safe and sound on a good sheltered ledge. So obviously it was from above that help must come, and the caravan trailed off to climb the Moucherotte by the path through the underbrush. Their worst fears had been set at rest, and if tears still ran from Mother's eyes, they were of joy and thankfulness.

Without the benefit of Wells' " time machine," let us now go back three hours, to the unhappy heroes of this adventure, hanging from the cliff like spiders at the end of their threads.

The cold had begun to numb their bruised and battered bodies; all suppleness had gone from their joints and their limbs were heavy and stiff. The silence they had worked so hard to combat was becoming steadily heavier. The Seyssins belfry tossed out its strokes with desperate slowness into the unending night; it was drizzling.

" Not even a cigarette ! " moaned André, the smoker of the party.

" Not even a match to break the darkness and give an instant's illusion of warmth," thought the others.

There was no doubt about it; the expedition had been most admirably planned right down to the smallest details.

Ten o'clock. The bivouackers, who had exhausted every means of distraction compatible with their situation, became aware of lights moving towards Saint Nizier from Grenoble; car headlamps were sweeping along the road they themselves had travelled ten hours before.

" Here come the rescue-parties," muttered someone.

" That's the end," growled Alain, " the absolute end. Twenty people putting themselves out and getting tired and upset and wet, all for nothing, because the minute it's light we can get out of this on our own. I can just see the edifying headlines in the papers tomorrow : ' Three inexperienced climbers disappear on the Moucherotte,' and all the good advice they'll hand out for ' those who are not accustomed to the mountains and their dangers,'—just as if you couldn't treat yourself to a bivouac." And Alain finished up with downright unfairness, " You know, it's absolutely impossible to do any climbing around Grenoble on *account of* the rescue-parties."

Jacques carried things a step further by reminding him that the Mountain Aid Committee could, by law, inflict a fine on anyone whose wantonly foolish behaviour necessitated the organising of search-parties. That was undoubtedly what would happen to them. They would have to face not only ridicule, but the prospect of a big bill as well.

" They'll be at the bottom in less than a couple of hours."

Silence fell again, but somehow it did not seem so bad now that they knew somebody was taking an interest in them and hurrying to help them bear the burden of loneliness. A very fine drizzle was still falling, so fine that it floated in the chill wind which was roaring against the cliff in great gusts. Twice since midnight the Seyssins belfry had speared the dark with single notes; it was one o'clock.

" They must be getting close."

The three concentrated their whole attention on the confused noises which rose from the valley through the mist, and suddenly the wind brought them what was, without any shadow of doubt, a hail from the very foot of the cliff which held them captive:

" Où où où où où . . ."

If only they had a light to show where they were, to allay the fears of the hagridden folk below, to tell them all was well, and above all (ye gods, above all) to get the hell out of it ! But there they were, without even a match between them, and the damned wind blowing in circles. Up on their feet and hanging at rope's end over the void, where they could see nothing but blackness, the three friends yelled in unison in an effort to make the rescuers understand. Through a final squall, they thought they heard them promise to come back. Then silence, heavier than ever, closed down again on the mountain.

This time sleep, allied with the cold, overcame them. Now and then one of them, dozing off, would pitch forward only to be brought up short by the rope, and the sleeper would awake with a start in all the terror of falling. They suffered death a thousand times over.

About three o'clock, Jacques became conscious of indistinct sounds from the top of the cliff; he turned and caught glimpses through the vanishing mist above the overhangs of a diffused halo of light which seemed to be moving along the crest of the Moucherotte. This will-o'-the-wisp really showed them for the first time the distance they were from their goal. (Good Lord, what a long way it still was to the summit !)

"Look, they're on the arête now."

Yes, they could hear faint shouting between the gusts of wind. They yelled with all their might in order to show their position to the rescuers, who succeeded after a number of tries in placing it pretty accurately. In a lull, they thought they heard something about sending down a bag of food and clothing.

"How on earth are they going to do that?" they wondered.

A few moments' wait; the reply was not long in coming. A hail of stones swept the cliff around them; the bombardment slackened for a second, then began again with renewed fury. It was a peculiarly unpleasant sensation, especially at dead of night. The bag, which was being let down to them on a rope, had far less chance of hitting them than one of the stones it was dislodging, and with one voice they implored their saviours not to bump them off, but just to let them be. Indistinctly from aloft came: "All right. We'll be back at dawn."

The stones stopped falling. The light vanished. Silence fell again like a thick black cloak.

Quarter past five. A murky light was spreading through the haze; it was a grey dawn. For the first time since the start of the bivouac the partners in distress could see where they were. True, none of them was a particularly beautiful sight; their faces were pinched and blue with cold, and their eyes, ringed and reddened by lack of sleep, strongly suggested "the morning after." While taking in busily every detail of the astounding perch where they had spent such a long and uncomfortable night, they rubbed away at their joints, which were so cramped that they would scarcely move, because obviously it was vital to escape the attentions of the rescue-party and finish the climb unaided.

Alas, their efforts were in vain; despite a quarter of an hour's massage their extremities remained useless, deadened and stiff. Besides, the ropes were in an inextricable tangle which their benumbed fingers could not cope with fast enough. They were still working at it when the rescuers, who had spent the night in the look-out post on the summit, reappeared on the edge. They stood, silhouetted against the sky, directly above the unfortunates they meant to save, willy-nilly, from their dizzy roost.

There was nothing else for it; with death in their hearts they roped themselves to the length of hemp let down by the head of the rescue-party, the devoted René Jamet, who, himself, climbed down over 300 feet to superintend operations. But, either from shame or pride, they made it a point of honour not to touch the safety-rope, which was left dangling; just the same, its moral support was probably not to be disdained. One by one, the three friends climbed the face, a very stiff proposition, which had resisted all Alain's efforts, and soon the only reminder of their stay in those airy regions was three little notches chiselled in a slab. And that corner of the cliff, which had been disturbed for twelve long hours by some of those annoying creatures called mountaineers, regained its thousand-year-old solitude.

Worn with anxiety, the parents watched their sons hoist themselves one after another, safe and sound, out of the gulf from which they had never thought to snatch them alive. They were so happy they simply had no heart to give them the scolding they felt they so richly deserved; Mother could hardly do more than whisper: "Darlings, we've been nearly frantic."

This morning the sky was completely clear. A pale October light streamed down over the Grésivaudan, all coppery with autumn tints, and upon the city below which was beginning to stir.

From the Forges valley the three companions stared for a long time at the wall they had scaled. Forefingers pointed out their route, and Alain the incorrigible, deploring its meanderings, asserted amid a disapproving silence: "We'll have to come back and do it again—straight up."

2. Up the Pic de la Fare (6.683 feet) by the Romanche slope

November 1st, 1943.

To anyone who goes up into the Oisans from Grenoble the valley between Vizille and Rochetaillée must seem quite devoid of charm. It is a deep ditch, shut in by steep banks, ploughed between Belledonne and the Taillefer. One leprous village follows another, each clustered about a sordid factory which not only soils the sky with its smoke but the Romanche with its outflow. What a sad end for the sacred waters of La Meije, Valfourche and the Vénéon!

Everywhere there are barrages, catchments, conduits and high-tension lines; Nature, which is well-fitted to raise man above himself, is nowhere so spoiled by his works.

However, at the far end of the ditch, where so much industrial ugliness ceases, the horizon smiles again; the whiteness of the Grandes-Rousses stands out against the sky. But before the two powerful riverside massifs of the Romanche relax their vice-like grip, Belledonne thrusts forward to dominate the torrent an immense rocky pyramid. This is the Pic de la Fare, whose summit shoots up over four thousand feet from the valley floor. Like an outpost it guards the Oisans from afar and tells its visitors, " Only a little way now and you will quit the dishonoured valley; you will soon see the shore of that massif whose very sight always makes your heart leap."

I do not know how many times I have travelled that road, but I never passed the foot of that peak, sprung straight out of some romantic engraving, without twisting my neck to try and probe the secret of its stern rock face. And immediately there would be let loose in me, like great gusts of desire, a passionate curiosity to get near those slabs and walls, and a burning need to be briefly master of that cliff so that I might remember it always.

I found, on enquiry, that the wall, though it had tempted many a seasoned mountaineer, was nevertheless still virgin; it was one more attraction had that been needed.

A ledge of enormous proportions, grassy and even wooded, cut right across the face about a fifth of the way up, and this bench should not be too hard to gain; from there it might be possible to scale one or other of the arêtes which bounded the cliff, preferably the eastern one. But these precipices distorted by the perspective are often full of surprises. As for forcing a way up the middle of the sheer, where the strata of the rock were twisted into scrolls and overhangs, it was unthinkable. On the extreme right the peak was split from top to bottom by an infernal couloir, as if it had received a terrific slash; there, too, it might be possible to find a route, despite some nasty projecting eaves, though this would be but a very poor alternative.

Two reconnaissances made on the way back from trips in the Oisans, somewhat half-heartedly, it is true, had failed to reach the vast bench, which nevertheless I considered as being merely the beginning of the difficulties. This romantic peak apparently claimed to be able to defend itself from foot to crest. Later, on a foggy Sunday in November 1938, I gained the summit with several friends, by slogging up some steep snow-covered slopes from the Voudène valley. Through a break in the mist, we had glimpsed the south face plunging down right from the peak to the Romanche, a disquieting abyss drowned in whirling wreaths, with fir-trees leaning their ghostly silhouettes towards it.

Another time I went up from Allemond as far as the Combe de Bâton to inspect the tempting cliff from the east, but before its steep profile I was hard put to it not to doubt. So, just as wolves circle incessantly about their prey before attacking, I ran rings untiringly around this mountain in search of its weak point. To launch a serious attempt on the peak, I should have to find not only a companion who would be interested in the trip, but also a favourable time. In summer there were better things to do; winter would mean certain failure, so it would definitely have to be between seasons.

Then came the war and the interruption of all our plans.

Autumn 1943. After the dolorous stupor of disaster, and our tremendous hope that France would find in her Calvary the means of her resurrection, we had seen with consternation the flight of the last driving forces from our unhappy country, torn further apart each day by her discords. And our great trials had begun. Little by little, the atmosphere grew heavier, charged with anguish. Our spirits, thirsty for truth, searched in vain for light in the confusion; our faith in the eternal destiny of France wavered. Never, as at that time, had the words " hope " and " duty " so clear a meaning for us. Never, too, had we felt so much need of pure air to soothe us, to calm the suspense of doing nothing and to relax our nerves, too long strained.

Our beloved mountains seemed to us then our greatest consolation, the only one capable of driving the obsession from our souls for a few hours, of making us forget our troubles and hardening the muscles softened by inaction. Let me admit that we also needed to re-discover a little pride in ourselves by doing some deed which was heroic in our own eyes. Despite the lateness of the season and the unfavourable weather, we had to measure ourselves against some savage cliff, where every yard of virgin ground gained must be bought with physical and mental effort capable of regenerating us.

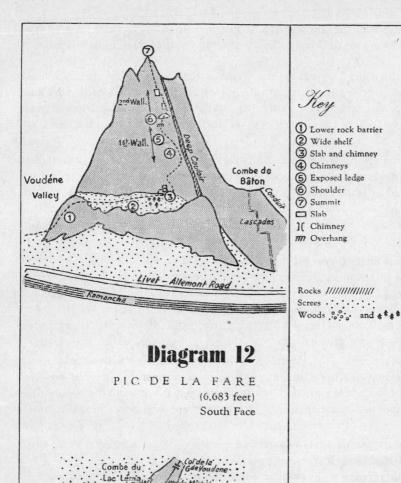

Key

① Lower rock barrier
② Wide shelf
③ Slab and chimney
④ Chimneys
⑤ Exposed ledge
⑥ Shoulder
⑦ Summit
▢ Slab
)(Chimney
𝑚 Overhang

Rocks //////////////
Screes · · · · · · ·
Woods ○·○·○· and ♠ ♣ ♠

Diagram 12

PIC DE LA FARE
(6,683 feet)
South Face

Timetable

Infernet Bridge	9.15 a.m.
Foot of the first wall	12.30 - 1 p.m.
Foot of the second wall	3.15 p.m.
Summit	4.30-4.45 p.m.
Livet	6.15 p.m.

And since the snow already put the high mountains out of the question, we decided to tackle the airy wall of the Pic de la Fare.

All Saints Day, 1943; the weather for the Feast of the Dead had come into line with the thoughts of the living. Mists floated like long shrouds in the Romanche valley; the sky above had drawn across its face the great black veil of its days of mourning, its days of rain.

We got off the train from Bourg d'Oisans at Livet about half-past eight, very dubious about the outcome of the trip; however, we could at least make a reconnaissance if nothing else. I was accompanied by Alain, my inseparable and indispensable leader, and one of his young friends, Rouchier, a tiro in the mountains, but really extremely gifted and filled with a burning passion for climbing.

The party traversed the village without much enthusiasm, whipped by a bitter and violent north wind; the weather was decidedly better suited to a visit to the cemetery than a mountain climb. Everything was saturated with moisture, sky, air and earth; it penetrated us to the marrow. Happily for them, the poor dead were not the only ones today who had to bear the weight of this damp icy ground !

We reached the Pointe de l'Infernet, where we stowed rucksacks and bicycles in a thicket. While we were about it, the weather improved little by little; " the sun escaped at last from the mountain's frozen fist," and managed by sheer perseverance to break through the layers of cloud. Thanks to that the rock would be almost dry.

It took only a few seconds' inspection of the rocky plinth, crowned by the big shelf, for my friend Alain to discover on the west side a broken track which would solve the problem of where to start. In the course of a previous, hastily-made reconnaissance I had been unable to gain the big bench, having run into some impossible and dangerous grassy overhangs. I had not found this track, which may not even have been in existence then. Today, thanks to the incomparable flair of my companion, we went swiftly and easily up a barely-perceptible goat-path, very airy and interrupted by climbs, but which in less than half an hour brought us to the giant balcony perched between two cliffs. In a rich meadow at the top, an enclosure built of stones bore witness to the sojourn in this lonely spot of some hermit shepherd.

Up to that point the expedition had been nothing but an easy walk, whereas we had expected to encounter difficulties right from the start. The sky now seemed to be on our side; great blue holes which spelled hope for us were appearing here and there in the vault of clouds. Some mists were still trailing through the valley, slow and heavy like sad thoughts.

The party hesitated a little about tackling the western edge of the face, but as I asserted my confidence, or rather my hope, in the practicability of the east side, my companions agreed to give it a try. We strode across the immense shelf, passing through rabbit-warrens, meadows and spinneys; above us rose the precipice, sheer, contorted and chiselled into undulating strata. Before we got to the end of the balcony, the upper wall, more broken here and less steep, was calling us irresistibly, and we decided to storm it right away instead of going further towards the east.

A few preparations at the foot of some attractive slabs, and the party became a cordée. Alain attacked immediately at good speed; we followed by means of some pleasant gymnastics. A few pitches brought us up to some nasty overhangs which it was useless to try; we looked for some other way. As it happened, there was a nice bush-covered ledge leading off to the right; in a few yards it took us to the foot of a long high rock slab up which a direct climb seemed likely to present serious difficulties. We had therefore to cross it slantwise and go up on the opposite side, at the point where it joined the cliff to form an angle.

Alain climbed with finger and toe-tips; his style was all delicacy. He did not fight the mountain with all his man's strength; he caressed it as gently as a sweetheart. Then suddenly, this extraordinary lover decided to use force; halfway up, he stopped on a slightly larger hold which he dignified by the name of "platform," and hit his darling as hard as he could—to drive in a piton, the rest of the pitch seeming to him very exposed. As soon as the karabiner had closed about the rope with a sharp snap, his caresses began again. At the limit of the grip of his espadrilles, our leader, legs open like a compass, stretched, drew himself out, clung to minute knobs, and finally got up to settle himself on a grassy balcony.

I had thought to follow his example in my nailed boots, but hardly had I climbed laboriously up a couple of yards, to the beginning of the traverse, than I realised the vanity of my pretensions. To punish me, since the rope was too short between Alain and me, I was condemned to change footgear in the middle of the pitch, not without trouble and the precious aid of our novice. To redeem this grave slur on my dignity, I strove to make the traverse with the maximum of ease and speed; our Benjamin crossed in his turn with plenty of skill and security indeed.

In order not to waste time on a narrow grassy platform, Alain at once began to scale the very wide chimney which dominated us. We could see him groping feverishly among the brush for holds worthy of the name, and battling furiously with the bushes that got in his way. Then we were strung out over that detestable terrain ourselves, nose and arms in the greenery where drops of the last rainfall still trembled. But the party soon reached the top of this first wall, and discovered that it was only a spur thrown off from the main cliff a little above. Just to the east, beyond a little ravine, some easy composite tiers, half-rock, half-vegetation, offered a chance of gaining eighty or a hundred yards of height without any trouble, and this semi-rustic passage was briskly made.

It was already half-past twelve, so we allowed ourselves several minutes' rest. While devouring our meagre provisions, we all agreed that the first part of our climb had perhaps been a false move; it looked as though it would in fact have been better and quicker to push further to the east along the big bench so as to miss our slabs, and climb straight up to the tiers we had just reached. We were now at the foot of the great precipice which formed the very crux of the problem to be solved, a cliff more than three hundred feet tall which shot up in a single burst.

Between mouthfuls, we looked at all the surroundings we should never see again—at least from here. In the mountains you must store up by every possible means all you can of the fleeting scenes which go to compose the alpine music in your memory. Far off, the Oisans melted into the greyness, the Rousses emerged like spectres from the mist. Opposite, the Taillefer and the Grand-Galbert lifted their heads, whitened by the icy blast of the north wind, while the brown tide of autumn submerged the forests which climbed their flanks. And there, right at the bottom, close to the thin trickle of water which was the Romanche, stretched a threadlike track where, mere children's toys, ran minute cars and harmless little trains.

We climbed rather more than half the wall, but the worst was undoubtedly yet to come. In order not to find ourselves benighted, we agreed to turn back between half-past three and four unless we were very close to the peak, so Alain, anxious to probe the secret of the cliff looming over us, attacked the base of the great wall without further delay.

The beginning was extremely encouraging, a succession of slabs of excellent rock, not too much tilted; there were just enough holds to make the climb interesting. The route we followed wormed its way between the buttresses like a snake in the grass; Alain instinctively spotted the key to each pitch at a glance. Not far to the right an immense gorge split the entire mountain; it was one of the routes we had envisaged, but quite the least stylish. The further we went, the steeper became the slant; our leader was soon going to come up against the foot of a projecting wall which might put paid to our attempt. But no, for he had guessed that the top of a couloir up which we had clambered for a few yards lower down would furnish a solution. This cleft in the rock did in fact narrow little by little to become first a chimney, then a crack; at the moment when it seemed about to vanish altogether, it suddenly bent over 45 degrees and turned its lower lip into a tiny rising ledge overlooking an abyss.

The party, taking advantage of this godsend, started along it, spread out to full length; we squeezed with some effort between the wall and the providential shrubs growing here and there, forming good natural belays. The climb was aerial and not without savour, but how we cursed as we hauled our rucksacks through the bushes! Then the ledge disappeared all of a sudden like a beautiful dream, but the worst seemed to be over. We did another grassy pitch suspended above a fascinating sheer drop, and came to a rocky overhang which necessitated an exposed "leg-up." Twice, for prudence sake, we had to use pitons, and the hours flew by like minutes; I kept looking anxiously at my wrist-watch.

Three o'clock already.

I began to have a sneaking feeling in the bottom of my heart that the trip would finish badly; the memory of a certain night in October 1932 spent on the wall of the Moucherotte came back to me like the acrid smell of stirred ashes. I had been mortified at the time by the deadly fear it had caused my parents, but I should feel even worse about it today if an unforeseen bivouac were to prostrate my wife, who would be more easily upset than usual since she was shortly expecting a child. As we climbed the easy tiers which terminated the great wall, I told my companion of the battle I was having with my conscience. Alain retorted with his customary superb confidence that the victory was practically won; we should be absolutely sure of that in a moment anyway, as soon as we could see beyond the wooded shoulder we were approaching, a real oasis of green suspended above the gulf.

Alas ! Three times alas ! From this untrodden bucolic spot we saw a new wall to be scaled, of a particularly disheartening aspect; the cliff to the left was vertical and not to be thought of, in the centre it was less steep but overlaid like the tiles on a roof, while on the right a succession of slabs separated by little ledges seemed to offer a path, however hazardous, across the wall. Close by, the deep and sinister gorge, already invaded by the night, ploughed a terrible furrow down the mountain. What an illustration for Dante's Inferno, '' All hope abandon, ye who enter here ! '' But there was no question of abandoning hope; we had to get out as fast as possible either by the top or the bottom.

It was already nearly four o'clock. According to our solemn pact, I proposed to give up the idea of conquering the last wall and to flee, by means of rappels, either back the way we had come or even by the horrific couloir. I had hardly set out this inglorious plan when Alain fairly exploded into imprecations, in which there was serious question as to whether anyone who boggled at sleeping-out in the mountains would not do better to put away ropes, axe and pitons and take up bowls, or, at a pinch, fishing. For his part, his decision was made, irrevocably; he was going home via the top, no matter what the risks. Our novice agreed tacitly.

So, as I had no particular liking for solitary mountaineering, I was forced to continue the ascent, from then on accursed. Now I can look back and bless the energy of the man who formed the real worth of our cordée, but at the time, anxiety, not about bivouacking but about frightening my family, nearly broke my heart. '' No, I simply haven't the right, just for the sake of my own pleasure. I must really give up all dangerous climbs . . .''

I can see any young readers who may have happened to pick up this book smiling over this vow and this shameful retreat. Well, all I can say is that you had better reap your harvest of success in the mountains before family responsibilities come to occupy your time, shackle your independence and invade your spirit. Later on, when you have a home brightened by the laughter of children, you too will know this intimate struggle between the call of the heights and your duty, your happiness, to stay with your own folk, and if, despite all, you go off to the mountains, then you will hear in the bottom of your heart the soft relentless voice of remorse.

During these internal lamentations, Alain was scaling the slabs with skill and rapidity; he had already covered the first pitch to a little platform. At top speed we joined him one after the other, then our whip placed a piton a few yards higher up under a projection which he negotiated quickly and stylishly. I followed, may I be forgiven, hauling on the rope as has never been done before, but I would have done anything to save time; our trip had become a real race with the clock, one eye constantly on our watches. The wall was prolonged by steep slopes of slippery rhododendrons, where several firs, which leaned over the gulf here and there, formed solid lifebuoys which you could shamelessly seize with open arms.

Quarter-past four. We could see another rocky barrier crowned with trees; would this really prove the last ? This illusion is so common on the mountains, that, in spite of my friend's unshakable confidence, I could not hide my black pessimism. The light was waning rapidly; our chances of escaping the dreaded bivouac grew slighter every minute. Vexation made me jumpy, oppressed me and squeezed my temples. To make matters worse, the weather was fast becoming menacing; bit by bit the cloud-ceiling had come down, drowning the neighbouring peaks, and now the summit of ours was in its turn submerged beneath the celestial tide. A few melting snowflakes began to fall. The cliffs were blurred through the mist and drizzle, the firs looked like ghosts; and at the same time the cold swooped down on the mountain.

One more tilted slab at whose foot our leader placed a piton; it was half-past four. He ascended it with dash, and we followed with all speed, solidly belayed by him. And then—then—we could not believe our eyes; the summit was there in the semi-darkness twenty yards above us. A rapid grassy slope and a final rocky barrier still separated us from it. It was almost at racing-pace that the cordée climbed the last glacis of the fortress ; the terminal chimneys scarcely reduced our speed, and at a quarter-to-five, in the falling night, we reached the peak, which was swept by a raging rain-charged wind.

An immediate relaxation relieved the pressure in my breast; I felt that I had been eased of an agony which crushed me like a cross.

The night, the rain and the mist mattered little now; by calling on my memory, I could lead my party back without let or hindrance via the Voudène valley, by the route I had followed five years before at the same season. We changed espadrilles for boots, and I started off smartly—towards the Combe de Bâton, glimpsed at the last moment in the gloaming between two banks of mist. Realised in time, this mistake had no grave consequences, unless it was having to run back a few yards to a little shoulder we had noticed beforehand through the greyness.

Now I recognised that I was on the right road, and we had only to hurry down the steep grass slopes of this side, which were divided by three or four fairly simple rocky barriers. Our only anxiety was not to miss the broken Voudène path, which should cross our line of march, under pain of ending up in some frightful schistous upheavals, from which we might never get out alive, and certainly not before tomorrow. Luckily the little track was faithful to the rendezvous I had mentally fixed for it, and through a forest all laden with damp odours the caravan returned at a quarter-past six to its base camp at the Pointe de l'Infernet.

So ended this short salutary escape; despite the anxiety which had gripped me I came back relaxed in body and soul to this sad, dull life where we struggle like wreckage in a high sea. That is why All Saints, 1943, in the long succession of hopeless days, will always seem to me like a blue patch in an inky sky.

February 1944.

I wrote those lines during the unhappy hours when France, in confusion, was smothering beneath the German yoke. In all honesty and sincerity I have not wished to alter a single word now that, thanks to the courage of her sons and her Allies, she has once more found her freedom and her place in the sun.

August 1944.

Chapter Eight

GONE WITH THE WIND

As I come to the end of this book it is to you, my life's partner, that I turn. What sadness and care have I not brought you by my too-ardent passion for the mountains ? None the less, you never complained; you even encouraged me, knowing the place it held despite everything in my heart. It was a real token of your love, perhaps a gentle indulgence too for that passion which was also yours and which brought us together. Just the same, you must have thought me a hardened egotist to go off as I have done, imposing upon you, for the sake of my own pleasure, the double burden of solitude and anxiety. But my soul has known many a conflict between that powerful call and my attachment to my little family circle.

Today I have come to a decision; my home has definitely won.

Here at any rate is what I ought to say :

" Goodbye, cliffs streaking upwards to the sky and the moraines; golden slabs which call to you; winding cracks which seize on you; goodbye, lovely pinnacles planted by God's own hand; snow-filled couloirs, the vertical roads up the mountains. Most of all goodbye, violent joy of the summit, explosion of long-restrained desire, and you, that sensation felt on the return journey, of bringing back with the victory a precious and tangible good. Goodbye; I take leave of you with regret but without bitterness, for twenty years of climbing have given me memories enough to last a lifetime. From now on I forbid myself this garden, but I shall know how to find in the lesser heights, with my family, joys every whit as pure even though less violent . . ."

Such would be the farewell that reason would compel me to make to the high mountains, to their temptations and their pleasures, their bondage and their danger. But even as I formulate it, I can feel dawning in myself the doubt—I had almost written the hope—as to whether I can keep such a promise without fail. The mountains are not something you can leave forever and never revisit. Ever-present memories, the alpine environment, the proximity of the peaks, all these form a magic circle from which no one can break at will.

So, readers, if you should happen to come across me up there despite this solemn farewell, try not to think too hardly of me, for as they say: " The spirit is willing but the flesh is weak."

PHOTOGRAPHS

GLOSSARY

ARÊTE
Steep mountain ridge

BELAY
Make the party safe by giving the rope a turn around some suitable projection. Also applied to the projection itself.

CHIMNEY
Fissure in rock or ice wide enough to admit the climber's body.

CORDÉE
Roped-together line of climbers.

CORNICHE
Overhanging snowbank formed by the wind on ridges.

COULOIR
Wide gully with rocky sides; there is usually ice or snow in the bottom.

CRACK
Fissure too narrow to admit climber's body.

CRAMPONS
Steel frame with spikes which can be fixed to boot for use on ice.

GENDARME
Solitary rock pinnacle.

GLISSADE
Controlled slide down snow-slopes.

ICEFALL
Very broken-up portion of glacier where it is descending sharply.

KARABINER
Steel snap-ring used to attach the rope to pitons.

NÉVÉ
Smooth, almost level, snowfield in upper section of glacier.

PITCH
Portion of climb between belays.

PITON
Steel spike which can be driven into rock or ice and used as hold or belay.

RAPPEL
Descent of steep slope by means of doubled rope around belay.

RIMAYE
Crevasse in glacier at the foot of a cliff.

ROTURE
Gaping void between a glacier and its rocky bank.

SÉRACS
Ice-pinnacles found in icefalls or steep ice slopes.